Test Book

DYNAMIC EARTH

Prentice Hall
Englewood Cliffs, New Jersey
Needham, Massachusetts

Test Book

PRENTICE HALL SCIENCE
Dynamic Earth

ISBN 0-13-987405-4

12 13 14 15   97 96 95

Prentice Hall
A Division of Simon & Schuster
Englewood Cliffs, New Jersey 07632

Contents

To the Teacher

This *Test Book* contains all the testing materials that accompany the student textbook. The testing materials are divided into three parts:

CHAPTER TEST

Every chapter in the student textbook has an accompanying Chapter Test. These tests are meant to test both factual recall and concept development. Each Chapter Test is divided into five sections. These sections are Multiple Choice, Completion, True or False, Using Science Skills, and Essay. An Answer Key for each Chapter Test is also included.

COMPUTER TEST BANK TEST

Every chapter in the student textbook has an accompanying Computer Test Bank Chapter Test. These tests are meant to test both factual recall and concept development. Each Computer Test Bank Test is divided into five sections. These sections are Multiple Choice, True or False, Completion, Using Science Skills, and Critical Thinking and Application. An Answer Key for each Test Bank Test is also included.

You may choose to copy the entire Computer Test Bank Chapter Test. A complete User's Guide is included in the disk package. Using your computer and the test disks, you can print out your own chapter test, quiz, midterm, or final exam, selecting questions from the Test Bank as well as adding your own. An Illustration Master for each visual question in the Test Bank Test is included after the questions. These Illustration Masters are to be used when you print out a test from your printer. An Answer Key for each test is also included.

The APPLE, IBM, and MAC disks for the ***Prentice Hall Science*** Computer Test Banks include questions from the Computer Test Bank for all 19 titles in the program.

For current prices and ordering information call your Customer Service Representative toll free 1-800-848-9500. Refer to the appropriate ISBN number below.

Item (ISBN #)	Description
0-13-987686-3	Apple 5 1/4-inch Program and Data Disks for the *Prentice Hall Science* Computer Test Bank (User's Guide included)
0-13-987702-9	IBM 5 1/4-inch Program and Data Disks for the *Prentice Hall Science* Computer Test Bank (User's Guide included)
0-13-986944-1	IBM 3 1/2-inch Program and Data Disks for the *Prentice Hall Science* Computer Test Bank (User's Guide included)
0-13-987694-4	MAC 3 1/2-inch Program and Data Disks for the *Prentice Hall Science* Computer Test Bank (User's Guide included)

PERFORMANCE-BASED TESTS

A set of Performance-Based Tests is included in this *Test Book*. Performance-Based Tests are designed to test a student's thinking and problem-solving abilities and are not meant to be content dependent. Although the tests have been designed to be given when the student has completed the textbook, you may prefer to give individual tests after particular chapters in the textbook. If you like, you may incorporate some of the Performance-Based Tests into your Chapter Test.

Performance-Based Tests are given at workstations. All materials the student needs are placed at the workstation, along with the worksheets the student must fill out. Students must be told in advance the amount of time they will have at each workstation. Make sure students understand that they must leave the workstation exactly as they found it.

Contents

Test Bank Test

CHAPTER 1 ■ Movement of the Earth's Crust

MULTIPLE CHOICE

Write the letter of the correct answer on the line at the left.

_____ **1.** When tension acts on rocks, the rocks are
  a. pushed together.
  b. pushed in two opposite, horizontal directions.
  c. tilted.
  d. pulled apart.

_____ **2.** When shearing acts on rocks, the rocks are
  a. pushed together.
  b. pushed in two opposite, horizontal directions.
  c. tilted.
  d. pulled apart.

_____ **3.** In a reverse fault, the hanging wall
  a. moves up relative to the foot wall.
  b. moves down relative to the foot wall.
  c. moves in the same direction as the foot wall.
  d. does not move.

_____ **4.** A fold is a
  a. fault.   c. joint.
  b. bend in a rock.   d. rift.

_____ **5.** An oval or circular uplifted area created by rising molten rock is called a
  a. fault-block mountain.   c. plateau.
  b. dome.   d. syncline.

_____ **6.** In a lateral fault, one block
  a. moves up relative to the other.
  b. slides over the other.
  c. moves horizontally past the other.
  d. breaks through the other.

_____ **7.** Deformation is
  a. the breaking of rocks.
  b. the tilting of rocks.
  c. the folding of rocks.
  d. any of these

_____ **8.** Mantle rocks
  a. are less dense than crust rocks.
  b. cannot move.
  c. float on crust rocks.
  d. flow slowly.

_____ 9. The Grand Canyon was formed by a river that cut through a
   a. plateau.   c. fault-block mountain.
   b. rift valley.   d. dome.

_____ 10. Movement of a block of rock along a fault
   a. is always upward.   c. is always sideways.
   b. is always downward.   d. can be upward, downward, or sideways.

COMPLETION

Complete each statement on the line at the left.

_____ 1. Parallel rock fractures that occur along numerous flat surfaces are called _____.

_____ 2. A fault that is formed when compression causes the hanging wall to move over the foot wall is called a(an) _____.

_____ 3. Rocks that bend easily are said to be _____.

_____ 4. A low area formed when a block of land between two normal faults slides downward is called a(an) _____.

_____ 5. The balancing of upward and downward forces that act between the two outermost layers of the Earth is called _____.

TRUE OR FALSE

Determine whether each statement is true or false. If it is true, write T. If it is false, change the underlined word or words to make the statement true.

_____ _____ 1. The outermost layer of the Earth is called the mantle.

_____ _____ 2. Mountains formed by blocks of rock uplifted by normal faults are called dome mountains.

_____ _____ 3. An upward fold is called a syncline.

_____ _____ 4. Molten rock found beneath the Earth's surface is called lava.

_____ _____ 5. The squeezing together of rocks by stress is called shearing.

USING SCIENCE SKILLS: Applying Concepts, Interpreting Diagrams

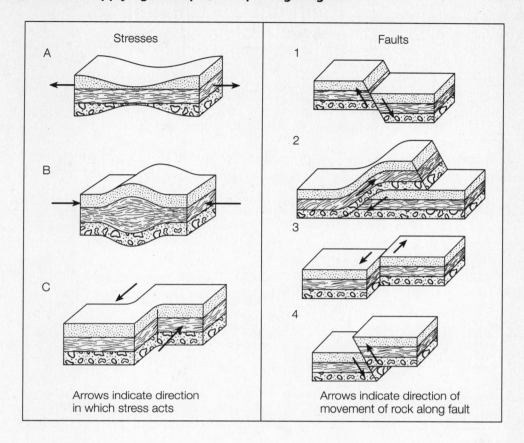

1. What kind of stress is illustrated in A?_____

   B? _____

   C? _____

2. Is the left wall or the right wall the hanging wall in 1? _____

   2? _____

   4? _____

3. What kind of fault is illustrated in 1?_____

   2? _____

   3? _____

   4? _____

4. What kind of stress accounts for the fault shown in 1? _____

    2? _____

    3? _____

    4? _____

ESSAY

Write a brief paragraph discussing each of the following statements or questions.

1. Explain in terms of forces how it is possible for water at the mouth of a river to remain at the same depth despite the fact that sediment is being deposited there.

_____

_____

_____

_____

_____

_____

_____

_____

_____

_____

2. Contrast the formation of fault-block mountains and dome mountains.

_____

_____

_____

_____

_____

_____

_____

_____

_____

_____

3. Describe two ways in which plateaus can be formed. How does the shape of a plateau

differ from that of a mountain? _____

_____

_____

_____

_____

_____

_____

_____

_____

_____

4. Contrast the two kinds of crust. _____

_____

_____

_____

_____

_____

_____

_____

_____

_____

_____

Answer Key

MULTIPLE CHOICE

1. d 2. b 3. a 4. b 5. b 6. c 7. d 8. d 9. a 10. d

COMPLETION

1. joints 2. thrust fault 3. ductile 4. rift valley 5. isostasy

TRUE OR FALSE

1. F, crust 2. F, fault-block mountains 3. F, an anticline 4. F, magma 5. F, compression

USING SCIENCE SKILLS

1. tension; compression; shearing 2. right wall; left wall; right wall 3. normal; thrust; lateral; reverse
4. tension; compression; shearing; compression

ESSAY

1. The extra sediment increases the weight of the Earth's crust, which floats on the mantle. This causes the downward force of the crust on the mantle to increase, which causes the crust to sink in order to reachieve a balance, or isostasy, relative to the upward force exerted by the mantle. Thus, the sinking of the crust and the depositing of sediments balance each other. Because the crust sinks at the same rate that sediments build up, the depth of the solid surface does not increase. 2. Fault-block mountains form when blocks of rock are lifted up by normal faults. Dome mountains form from domes, which result from an uplift of a circular or oval area due to rising magma that pushes upward without erupting. If the domes wear away, exposing separate peaks of hardened magma, dome mountains result. 3. Plateaus can be formed when forces slowly push horizontally on an area, causing uplift. They can also be formed by a series of lava flows that spread out, fill in areas, harden, and build up. Plateaus, unlike mountains, are flat-topped rather than peaked. 4. Continental crust makes up the Earth's landmasses. Oceanic crust is found under the ocean floor. Continental crust tends to be thicker than oceanic crust (roughly 32 km thick versus roughly 8 km thick).

Test Bank Test

CHAPTER 1 ■ Movement of the Earth's Crust

MULTIPLE CHOICE

Write the letter of the answer that best completes each statement.

_____ 1. A force that greatly deforms rocks is
   a. cleavage.   c. conduction.
   b. deflation.   d. stress.

_____ 2. Compression differs from tension because
   a. compression pushes rocks in opposite directions.
   b. tension squeezes rocks together.
   c. compression squeezes rocks together.
   d. tension pushes rocks in opposite directions.

_____ 3. When joints form in rocks, they
   a. are parallel to each other.
   b. intersect each other at 90 degrees.
   c. radiate out in a star pattern.
   d. form only as reverse faults.

_____ 4. Which of these processes will *not* deform the Earth's crust?
   a. uplifting   c. red shift
   b. shearing   d. stress

_____ 5. The crust of the Earth
   a. is stable and uniformly stationary in one spot above the Earth's outer core.
   b. floats on outer core rock.
   c. is cemented to the Moho and does not move.
   d. floats on the mantle.

_____ 6. Isostasy in the Earth occurs because
   a. oxygen and iron combine to form a heavy metal.
   b. pressures of the mantle and crust are opposite, balancing forces.
   c. thrust faults act vertically.
   d. carbon dioxide is utilized in the formation of plant materials.

_____ 7. If the tons of ice that cover the Antarctic were to melt, the crust in that area would
   a. sink lower on the core.   c. float higher on the mantle.
   b. remain virtually unchanged. d. be compressed and squeezed.

_____ 8. Massive amounts of sediments deposited in the Gulf of Mexico have caused the
   a. formation of guyots.
   b. floor of the Gulf to develop a rift.
   c. development of a moraine.
   d. floor of the Gulf to sink.

_____ 9. Thrust faults develop because
   a. tension causes the foot wall to rise above the hanging wall.
   b. shearing occurs in horizontal rock layers.
   c. compression lowers the hanging wall of a fault.
   d. compression forces the hanging wall over the foot wall of a fault.

_____ 10. Rocks have been carried many kilometers from their original location by
   a. thrust faults.   c. joints.
   b. reverse faults.   d. normal faults.

_____ 11. A fault is a
   a. horizontal force acting on a rock layer.
   b. folding of rocks.
   c. break along which rocks move.
   d. pushing of rock in a vertical direction.

_____ 12. When a fault occurs,
   a. sediments are deposited under parent rock.
   b. stress is released.
   c. rocks bend but do not break.
   d. rocks double their ductility.

_____ 13. Rocks will probably fold if they
   a. are ductile.   c. undergo sudden stress.
   b. experience rapid cooling. d. are brittle.

_____ 14. Plateaus result from
   a. horizontal forces.
   b. the faulting of cold rock layers.
   c. the rising and cooling of magma.
   d. the deposition of tons of sediment.

_____ 15. The Columbia Plateau developed from
   a. faulting of rock layers.   c. lava flows.
   b. an uplift of rock beds.   d. folding of sediments.

_____ 16. Domes differ from plateaus because they
   a. are formed from molten magma.
   b. occur in the Earth's crust.
   c. are formed from rising magma that does not erupt on the surface.
   d. appear as depressions in the Earth's crust.

_____ 17. Domes that have been eroded away form peaks called
   a. fault peaks.   c. joint peaks.
   b. dome valleys.   d. dome mountains.

_____ 18. When domes form,
   a. the rock layers of the surrounding area stay flat.
   b. the rock layers over the dome area remain flat and in place.
   c. lava pours out horizontally on the surface of the Earth.
   d. reverse faults produce a rift valley over the dome site.

_____ 19. Older rocks are found on top of younger rocks in
   a. joints.   c. normal faults.
   b. thrust faults.   d. reverse faults.

_____ **20.** A thrust fault results in
    a. a hanging wall moving down relative to the foot wall.
    b. the foot wall sliding sideways relative to the hanging wall.
    c. the hanging wall sliding over the foot wall.
    d. the foot wall sliding over the hanging wall.

_____ **21.** The Columbia Plateau is *not* located in
    a. Colorado.   c. Idaho.
    b. Oregon.   d. Washington.

_____ **22.** Surface lava flowing on the Earth's surface resulted in the formation of the
    a. Black Hills Plateau.   c. Appalachian Plateau.
    b. Colorado Plateau.   d. Columbia Plateau.

_____ **23.** Tension in Earth materials causes
    a. the squeezing of rocks together.
    b. rocks to be pulled apart.
    c. rocks to be pushed in two opposite, horizontal directions.
    d. fault blocks to form in rocks.

_____ **24.** Anticlines form as a result of
    a. a downward fold in rock layers.
    b. a hanging wall being pushed above a foot wall.
    c. an upward fold in rock beds.
    d. compression forcing a foot wall over a hanging wall.

_____ **25.** Rift valleys form when
    a. two blocks move horizontally past one another.
    b. rock beds fold downward.
    c. a block between two normal faults slides downward.
    d. a hanging wall slides over a foot wall.

_____ **26.** Faulting differs from folding because
    a. shearing occurs in folding.   c. faulting bends but does not break rock.
    b. rocks bend in folding.   d. faulting always produces anticlines.

_____ **27.** Synclines are like anticlines because
    a. they have two normal faults.
    b. they each contain rift valleys.
    c. both result from magma deposits on the surface of the Earth.
    d. they both contain folds.

_____ **28.** If you walked to the center of an anticline, you would be standing
    a. on a normal fault.   c. on a hill.
    b. in a rift valley.   d. on a foot wall.

_____ **29.** If force is applied to rock beds gradually, they will most likely
    a. form fault blocks.   c. develop lateral faults.
    b. develop folds.   d. form a rift valley.

_____ **30.** When rocks are subjected to continual stress, their
      a. volume changes but their shape remains the same.
      b. shape changes but their density remains the same.
      c. density changes but their volume remains unchanged.
      d. volume changes and their shape changes.

TRUE OR FALSE

Determine whether each statement is true or false.

_____ **31.** The pushing and pulling of the Earth's crust is called deformation.

_____ **32.** Shearing pushes crustal rock in two opposite horizontal directions.

_____ **33.** Earthquakes often occur in faults in the Earth's crust.

_____ **34.** The difference between a normal fault and a reverse fault is that in a normal fault, the hanging wall moves up relative to the foot wall.

_____ **35.** Valleys formed when the block of land between two normal faults slides downward are called rift valleys.

_____ **36.** A bend in a rock layer is called a joint.

_____ **37.** If rocks become extremely hot during compression, they are more likely to fault than to fold.

_____ **38.** Plateaus are layers of flat-topped rocks high above sea level that cover large areas of land.

_____ **39.** An uplifted area created by magma from below is called a hill or mound.

_____ **40.** The crust of the Earth floats because mantle rock is less dense than crustal rock.

COMPLETION

Fill in the word or number that best completes each statement.

_____ **41.** The _____ of the Earth is usually 8 km thick, and is found under the ocean floor.

_____ **42.** The layer of the Earth called the _____ is made of rock that flows slowly.

_____ **43.** The _____ is the block of rock above a fault.

_____ **44.** If a stress due to compression is acting on a fault, the hanging wall will move up relative to the foot wall in a _____ fault.

_____ **45.** Blocks of rock uplifted by normal faults are called _____ mountains.

_____ **46.** When a block of land between two normal faults slides downward, a _____ valley is formed.

_____ **47.** Layers of rock that bend can produce a downward fold known as a _____.

_____ **48.** Rock type, force, pressure, and _____ are four factors that determine whether rocks will fold or fault.

_____ **49.** A _____ is a large, flat-topped area, often near folded mountains, that is not faulted or folded.

_____ **50.** An upward fold in a rock bed is called a(an) _____.

_____ **51.** The plateau that covers parts of the states of Oregon, Washington, and Idaho is called the _____ plateau.

_____ **52.** A _____ is an uplifted area on the surface of the Earth that looks like the top half of a large sphere, and is caused by magma rising from within the Earth.

_____ **53.** A balance called _____ occurs when the upward force of the mantle and the downward force of the crust are equal.

_____ **54.** Sandstone is a rock that is very _____ and will break easily when a force is applied.

_____ **55.** Ductile rocks are more likely to _____ while brittle rocks are more likely to fault.

_____ **56.** A _____ fault is one along which the blocks of rock move horizontally past each other.

_____ **57.** The crust of the ocean floor will _____ downward if massive sediments are deposited on top of the floor.

_____ **58.** When compression within the Earth causes a hanging wall to slide over a foot wall, a _____ fault will result.

_____ **59.** A _____ wall differs from a hanging wall in that it is the block below the fault.

_____ **60.** Any bend in a rock when stress is applied is called a _____.

Use the skills you have developed in the chapter to answer each question.

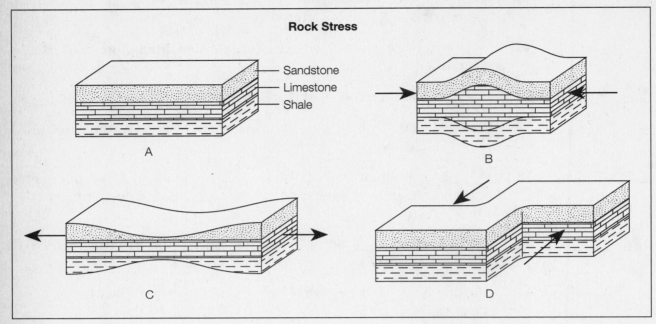

Figure 1

61. Describe the rock unit shown in Figure 1, diagram A.

62. Compare diagram B in Figure 1 to diagram A. How is it different?

63. Based on the evidence shown in diagram B of Figure 1, what type of fault will form if the forces at work continue to exist?

64. What caused the sandstone to take on the shape shown in diagram C of Figure 1?

65. In Figure 1, how does the stress in diagram C differ from the stress in diagram B?

66. Will a normal fault result from the stresses being applied to the rock unit in diagram D of Figure 1? Explain.

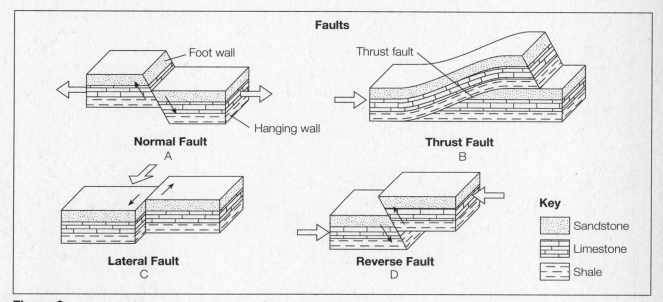

Figure 2

67. In Figure 2, describe the movement that occurred to produce the fault in diagram A.

68. How do the movements of the fault in diagram D of Figure 2 compare with those of the fault in diagram C?

69. Based on the evidence shown in diagram C of Figure 2, will a hanging wall and foot wall develop? Explain.

70. Which diagrams in Figure 2 have stress forces being applied in the same direction?

71. What type of rock is exposed on the foot wall of the fault in diagram A of Figure 2?

CRITICAL THINKING AND APPLICATION

Discuss each of the following in a brief paragraph.

72. Create a diagram that shows three sedimentary rock layers folded into two anticlines with a syncline between them. Label the three structures.

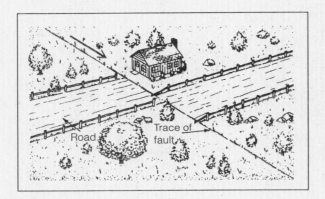

Figure 3

73. Study the sketch in Figure 3. Using evidence that you can gather from the sketch, explain any crust movement that has occurred at this site.

74. Reverse faults, normal faults, lateral faults, thrust faults, anticlines, and synclines are types of Earth movement. Which of these are evident in Figure 4?

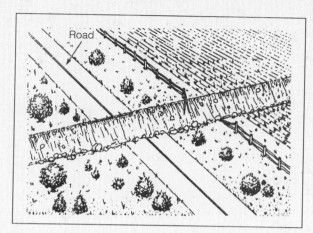

Figure 4

75. Interstate highway 21, a busy thoroughfare, runs north and south through the town of Jonesville. Last night at 11:00 PM, an earthquake occurred along a fault that runs across the highway from east to west. A hanging wall 3 m high was pushed up on the north side of the fault. The roadbed shifted laterally, causing the south side of the fault to move 12 m to the left. Local authorities have many problems to face. Can you identify some of these problems and offer possible solutions?

76. How can rock in the Earth be both brittle and ductile?

77. Are all rock folds anticlines? Explain.

78. Explain the difference between a fault and a fold.

79. Describe one way in which a plateau can form.

80. Compare a lateral fault to a normal fault.

81. In what ways is a dome different from a plateau?

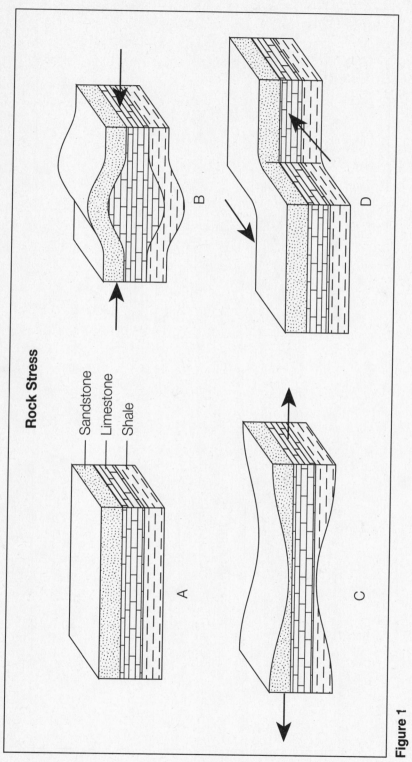

Rock Stress

Sandstone
Limestone
Shale

A

B

C

D

Figure 1

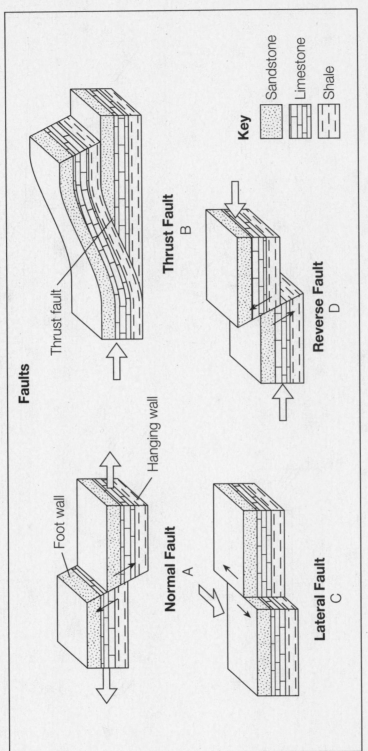

Figure 2

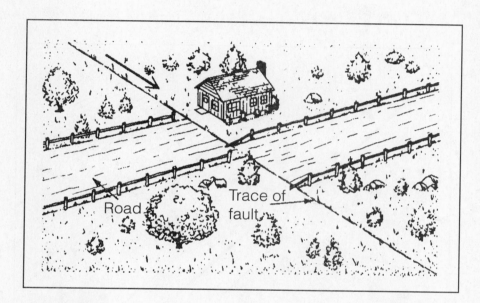

Figure 3

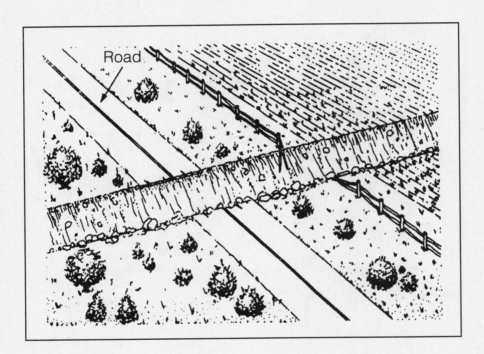

Road

Figure 4

Test Bank Answer Key

1. d
2. c
3. a
4. c
5. d
6. b
7. c
8. d
9. d
10. a
11. c
12. b
13. a
14. c

15. c
16. c
17. c
18. a
19. b
20. c
21. a
22. d
23. b
24. c
25. c
26. b
27. d
28. c

29. b
30. d
31. F
32. T
33. T
34. F
35. T
36. F
37. F
38. T
39. F
40. F

41. crust
42. mantle
43. hanging wall
44. reverse
45. fault-block
46. rift
47. syncline
48. temperature
49. plateau
50. anticline
51. Columbia
52. dome
53. isostasy
54. brittle
55. fold
56. lateral
57. sink
58. thrust
59. foot
60. fold
61. Diagram A shows a section of rock that contains three different layers. The layers are sandstone on top, followed by limestone and shale. All layers are parallel and are equal in thickness. There are no forces being exerted on this rock unit.
62. Diagram B shows that the three layers present are experiencing compression, causing the layers to bulge in the center. The surface has an anticline which is absent in diagram A, and the shale layer has a syncline.
63. reverse fault
64. tension stress
65. In diagram C the rocks are stretched like a piece of taffy. In diagram B the rocks are pushed together, causing a bulge higher up and deeper down.
66. No, because the stresses being applied will not push the rock unit up or down but sideways, and a lateral fault will develop.

67. Tension stress causes the rock unit to separate in opposite directions. As this occurs, the hanging wall slides down relative to the foot wall.
68. The movements in both cases are along the fault itself. The movements differ in direction. The lateral fault movement is horizontal, while the movement of the reserve fault is vertical.
69. No, because a hanging wall and foot wall require vertical motion of the rock unit.
70. B and C
71. sandstone and limestone
72. Check students' diagrams.
73. The sketch shows a rural area with a road passing from right to left. A lateral fault has occurred, causing the ground to shift horizontally along the fault line. The shifted roadbed and fine line crossing the road are evidence that a fault has occurred.
74. A normal fault has occurred because the foot wall in the background has been lifted up to form a slope. In addition, a small amount of lateral fault movement has occurred because the road in the foreground has been shifted to the right.
75. Normal traffic: set up roadblocks to reroute traffic around affected area. Future earthquake activity: consult seismologist and highway department about safety. Rise in roadway: bulldoze to level the ground.
76. Rocks that make up the Earth respond to external forces in different ways depending on the type of force being applied. If great and continuous compression forces are applied to rock layers over a long period of time, the rock layers will become ductile and will bend and fold. However, if a severe instantaneous shearing force is applied, the layers will snap and break because they are far too brittle to withstand the instant force. Also, the composition of individual rock types affects whether they are brittle or ductile.
77. No. Only upward folds in rock layers are anticlines. Rock layers may have both upward and downward folds present in the same rock unit.
78. A fault is a break or crack in rock layers along which rocks move. A fold is a bend in the rock layers.
79. Student answers may vary. A plateau may form as a result of horizontal forces that push on an area, causing the area to rise while the rock layers remain flat. Plateaus may also form from a series of lava flows that pour out onto the surface of the Earth and harden into horizontal layers.
80. In both a lateral and normal fault, movement of the Earth occurs along the fault line. Normal faults result from tension and produce a vertical hanging wall and foot wall. Lateral faults result form shearing forces that cause blocks of the Earth to slide horizontally past each other.
81. A dome is much smaller than a plateau. The rock layers in a dome are folded. The rock layers in a plateau are flat and unfolded. Domes are formed by magma (or other materials) pushing up beneath existing rock layers and bending them into a hill. Plateaus may be formed by the buildup of materials as well as by uplifting.

Contents

Chapter Test

CHAPTER 2 ■ Earthquakes and Volcanoes

MULTIPLE CHOICE

Write the letter of the correct answer on the line at the left.

_____ 1. Which of the following cause particles to move back and forth in the direction the waves are moving?
a. P waves   c. S waves
b. L waves   d. tsunamis

_____ 2. The most common cause of earthquakes is
a. volcanoes.   c. weather.
b. faulting.   d. tsunamis.

_____ 3. Which of the following is formed from lava whose chemical composition is similar to that of both light-colored and dark-colored lava?
a. rhyolite   c. andesite
b. pumice   d. basalt

_____ 4. Which of the following is made up of particles about the size of grains of rice?
a. volcanic ash   c. cinders
b. volcanic bombs   d. volcanic dust

_____ 5. Which of the following is made up of particles about the size of golf balls?
a. volcanic ash   c. cinders
b. volcanic bombs   d. volcanic dust

_____ 6. Quiet flows of runny lava produce
a. composite volcanoes.   c. cinder cones.
b. shield volcanoes.   d. calderas.

_____ 7. In a year, the number of earthquakes that cause severe changes in the Earth's surface is about
a. 3.   c. 10.
b. 5.   d. 20.

_____ 8. Which of the following is located on a major earthquake and volcano zone?
a. Norway   c. Denmark
b. Sweden   d. Iceland

_____ 9. Cinder cones result from
a. alternating layers of rock particles and lava.
b. lava flows.
c. quiet eruptions of rock particles.
d. explosive eruptions of rock particles.

_____ 10. The San Andreas fault is located in
a. Spain.   c. California.
b. Mexico.   d. Texas.

COMPLETION

Complete each statement on the line at the left.

_____ 1. Scientists who study earthquakes are called _____.

_____ 2. The strength of earthquakes is measured according to a scale called the _____.

_____ 3. A great sea wave is called a(an) _____.

_____ 4. The point on the Earth's surface directly above an earthquake's point of origin is called the _____.

_____ 5. An instrument that detects and measures seismic waves is called a(an) _____.

TRUE OR FALSE

Determine whether each statement is true or false. If it is true, write T. If it is false, change the underlined word or words to make the statement true.

_____ _____ 1. The underground point of origin of an earthquake is called the epicenter.

_____ _____ 2. L waves are surface waves.

_____ _____ 3. The fastest moving seismic waves are S waves.

_____ _____ 4. A warning signal that can be used to predict earthquakes is rising of land near a fault.

_____ _____ 5. Secondary waves cannot travel through liquids.

USING SCIENCE SKILLS: Applying Concepts; Making Comparisons

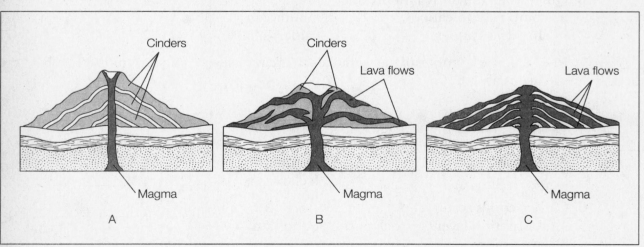

1. Which type of volcano is illustrated by A?_____

   B? _____

   C? _____

2. What kind of eruption—quiet, explosive, or both at different times—would be expected

from A? _____

B? _____

C? _____

3. Which type of volcano would tend to produce basalt? _____

How can you tell? _____

_____

4. Which type of volcano is Mount Vesuvius? _____

Mauna Loa? _____

Paricutín? _____

ESSAY

Write a brief paragraph discussing each of the following statements or questions.

1. Contrast the types of lava that produce rhyolite, andesite, basalt, and scoria.

_____

_____

_____

_____

_____

_____

2. Why are volcanoes considered "windows" into the interior of the Earth?

_____

_____

_____

_____

_____

_____

_____

3. Name and compare the three main types of seismic waves. _____

_____

_____

_____

_____

_____

_____

4. Explain the structure and operation of a seismograph. _____

_____

_____

_____

_____

_____

_____

Answer Key

MULTIPLE CHOICE

1. a **2.** b **3.** c **4.** a **5.** c **6.** b **7.** a **8.** d **9.** d **10.** c

COMPLETION

1. seismologists **2.** Richter scale **3.** tsunami **4.** epicenter **5.** seismograph

TRUE OR FALSE

1. F, focus **2.** T **3.** F, P waves **4.** T **5.** T

USING SCIENCE SKILLS

1. cinder cone; composite; shield **2.** explosive; both at different times; quiet **3.** C. Basalt is formed from runny lava, which is produced by shield volcanoes. **4.** B (composite); C (shield); A (cinder cone)

ESSAY

1. Lava that produces rhyolite is light-colored, contains little water, and can cause explosive eruptions. Lava that produces andesite has a chemical composition similar to that of both dark- and light-colored lava. Lava that produces basalt is dark-colored, contains much water, is thin and runny, and tends to flow quietly. Lava that produces scoria contains large amounts of gases. **2.** Volcanoes release lava through vents. By analyzing the mineral makeup of the lava, geologists can determine the chemical composition of the magma within the Earth from which the lava came. **3.** Primary (P) waves are the fastest moving; can travel through solids, liquids, and gases; and cause rock particles to move back and forth in the same direction the waves are moving. Secondary (S) waves are slower moving, cannot travel through liquids and gases, and cause rock particles to move at right angles to the direction of the waves. Surface (L) waves are the slowest moving, move along the Earth's surface after traveling up to the epicenter, and cause most of the damage during an earthquake. **4.** A seismograph consists of a pen attached to a weight that is, in turn, attached to a spring or wire. The pen marks a sheet of paper that is wound around a rotating drum that moves with the Earth. Movement of the drum results in production of a wavy line, which indicates movement of the Earth.

Test Bank Test

CHAPTER 2 ■ Earthquakes and Volcanoes

MULTIPLE CHOICE

Write the letter of the answer that best completes each statement.

_____ 1. Earthquakes result from
    a. lava flows that solidify on the surface of the Earth's crust.
    b. cinders being blown into the atmosphere.
    c. sudden movements of part of the Earth's crust.
    d. tsunamis that crash into shorelines.

_____ 2. Earthquake waves can be simulated by
    a. throwing a rock up in the air.
    b. pouring water into an empty pan.
    c. allowing a cake mix to flow across a baking pan.
    d. throwing a rock into a pond.

_____ 3. The focus of an earthquake is
    a. a spot on the surface of the Earth where an earthquake originates.
    b. at the surface of the ocean where P waves begin.
    c. located where the fault line appears at the Earth's surface.
    d. beneath the Earth's surface where the rocks break and move.

_____ 4. In most cases, earthquakes are caused by
    a. folding.   c. faulting.
    b. isostasy.   d. erosion.

_____ 5. P waves from an earthquake
    a. are the slowest waves.
    b. arrive at a given point before other seismic waves.
    c. cause the most damage.
    d. always arrive at a given point after S waves.

_____ 6. S waves
    a. travel through solids, liquids, and gases.
    b. travel through liquids but not solids.
    c. travel through solids but not liquids.
    d. do not travel through solids and liquids.

_____ 7. During earthquakes, the most violent shaking occurs
    a. in cities.   c. where P waves and S waves meet.
    b. at the focus.   d. at the epicenter.

_____ 8. The San Andreas fault movement in 1906 caused
    a. a great tsunami that came ashore at San Francisco and did tremendous damage.
    b. an earthquake.
    c. a volcano.
    d. a midocean ridge that emerged at Los Angeles.

_____ **9.** A tsunami is caused by
   a. folding of rock layers.   c. an earthquake.
   b. lava flows from a volcano.   d. the erosion and collapse of sea cliffs.

_____ **10.** S waves differ from P waves because they
   a. cause rocks to move at right angles to the waves.
   b. are faster than P waves.
   c. pass through solids, liquids, and gases.
   d. speed up as they pass through more dense material in the Earth.

_____ **11.** The slowest of the earthquake waves are the
   a. S waves.   c. P waves.
   b. L waves.   d. A waves.

_____ **12.** An operating seismograph is an instrument that has a
   a. pen attached by a wire to a rotating drum.
   b. weighted drum that does not move when the Earth shakes.
   c. weight that does not move during an earthquake.
   d. stationary drum attached to a heavy weight that does not move.

_____ **13.** According to the Richter scale, a very destructive earthquake would have a magnitude equal to or greater than
   a. −2.   c. 10.
   b. 6.   d. 100.

_____ **14.** An operating seismograph that sits motionless and suddenly receives a P wave from an earthquake records a line that is
   a. wavy.
   b. a straight line followed by a wavy line.
   c. straight.
   d. a wavy line followed by a straight line and another wavy line.

_____ **15.** According to the Richter scale, an earthquake with a magnitude of 4 is how many times stronger than an earthquake with a magnitude of 2?
   a. 10 times   c. 100 times
   b. 20 times   d. 40 times

_____ **16.** A seismologist is a specialist who
   a. studies the history of the Earth.
   b. studies faults and how the Earth's crust moves along those faults.
   c. helps people make the best use of land without harming it.
   d. inspects mineral resources and ensures that safety regulations are followed in their use.

_____ **17.** Using the Richter scale, which of these earthquake magnitudes indicates that an earthquake is very destructive?
   a. 2   c. 7
   b. 4   d. −6

_____ **18.** The amount of damage caused by an earthquake does not depend on the
   a. strength of the quake.
   b. distance the seismograph stations are located from the epicenter.
   c. population of the quake area.
   d. strength of the buildings in the quake area.

_____ **19.** A warning signal that will not help us predict earthquakes in an area is
   a. a drop in the height of land near a fault.
   b. the rise and fall of water in a well.
   c. a change in speeds of incoming P and S waves.
   d. an abrupt change in barometric pressure.

_____ **20.** The difference between lava and magma is that
   a. lava is not melted rock.
   b. magma is igneous and lava is not.
   c. lava reaches the Earth's surface and magma does not.
   d. magma reaches the Earth's surface and lava does not.

_____ **21.** A volcanic eruption is
   a. an intensity of 7 measured on the Richter scale.
   b. a giant sea wave with destructive force.
   c. a tremendous fault block mountain resulting from two separate faults.
   d. a discharge of lava from an Earth vent.

_____ **22.** A volcano is a "window" into the Earth because
   a. through the opening of volcano, scientists can travel into the Earth's interior.
   b. extinct volcanoes leave a cool, open tunnel into the Earth through which studies of the Earth's deep interior can be accomplished.
   c. materials ejected by a volcano can give scientists clues about the Earth's interior.
   d. scientific research equipment lowered many kilometers through volcanic openings has provided valuable data about the outer core of the Earth.

_____ **23.** Rhyolite is a hardened form of lava that
   a. resembles granite, is light in color, and contains silica.
   b. is dark in color and is rich in iron and magnesium.
   c. contains abundant gases that form holes in the rock and is either dark or light in color.
   d. contains a lot of water and is rich in iron and carbon dioxide.

_____ **24.** Pumice is different from basalt because it
   a. is dark and very heavy.   c. lacks silica.
   b. contains a lot of gas bubbles. d. lack gas bubbles.

_____ **25.** Dark-colored lava
   a. is thin and runny.   c. contains no water.
   b. is thick and lumpy.   d. is very noisy as it flows from a volcano.

_____ **26.** While observing and studying a volcano in Hawaii, you captured some of the volcanic material falling from the air. If the material all measured at least 1.0 mm in size, you would correctly classify them as
   a. cinders.   c. volcanic dust.
   b. volcanic bombs.   d. volcanic ash.

_____ **27.** Materials the size of golf balls hurled from an active volcano would be classified as
   a. ash.   c. cinders.
   b. cones.   d. dust.

b. cones. d. dust.

_____ 28. One of the most famous composite volcanoes is
    a. Paricutín in Mexico. c. Kilauea in Hawaii.
    b. Izalco in El Salvador. d. Mount Etna in Italy.

_____ 29. The Ring of Fire zone includes
    a. New Zealand, the Philippines, and Japan.
    b. Italy, Greece, and Turkey.
    c. Iceland.
    d. Asia and India.

_____ 30. To measure an earthquake, you would use a
    a. barometer. c. balance.
    b. graduated cylinder. d. seismograph.

TRUE OR FALSE

Determine whether each statement is true or false.

_____ 31. Earthquakes result from folding, which is a break in the Earth's crust.

_____ 32. A giant sea wave called a tsunami can be created as a result of vibration from an earthquake.

_____ 33. The epicenter is the underground point of origin of an earthquake.

_____ 34. The Van Allen scale measures the strength of earthquakes.

_____ 35. An earthquake that measures a 5 on the Richter scale is ten times stronger than an earthquake that measures a 4 on the same scale.

_____ 36. Shields are volcanic bombs the size of golf balls that are hurled from a volcano during an eruption.

_____ 37. Mauna Loa in Hawaii is the largest known shield volcano.

_____ 38. When the top of a volcano collapses or explodes, a caldera forms at the site of the volcano.

_____ 39. The material that composes a cinder cone volcano is very solidly packed, giving the volcano considerable height.

_____ 40. Lava is classified only in two distinct categories.

COMPLETION

Fill in the word or number that best completes each statement.

_____ 41. The majority of earthquakes that occur are due to _____.

_____ 42. During an earthquake, the _____ is the location of the most intense shaking of the Earth.

_____ 43. When a violent break in the Earth's crust occurs, the vibrations produce a(an) _____ which shakes houses, trees, and other objects on the surface of the Earth.

_____ 44. An earthquakes's strength on the _____ scale is calculated from the

_____ **45.** The _____ of an earthquake is the point beneath the Earth's surface where the rocks break and move.

_____ **46.** There are _____ main types of seismic waves associated with earthquakes.

_____ **47.** The fastest of the main seismic waves are the _____ waves.

_____ **48.** Most of the damage to cities and towns during an earthquake comes from _____ waves.

_____ **49.** Seismographs produce a _____ during an earthquake to record the waves that develop.

_____ **50.** The amount of damage caused by an earthquake will be determined by the _____ of the earthquake.

_____ **51.** Within the Earth, rock exists as a hot liquid called _____.

_____ **52.** Once hot, liquid rock reaches the surface of the Earth, it is known as _____.

_____ **53.** The opening or _____ in the Earth's crust is the location where hot, liquid rock spills out onto the surface of the Earth.

_____ **54.** Volcanic lava that is _____ in color is rich in iron and magnesium.

_____ **55.** Rhyolite-forming lava contains _____, which is responsible for its light color.

_____ **56.** The three types of volcanoes are the _____ cone, shield, and _____ volcano.

_____

_____ **57.** Mt. Vesuvius in Italy is classified as a _____ volcano.

_____ **58.** Volcanoes may develop a _____ or pit at the top.

_____ **59.** In _____ volcano formation, eruptions are usually quiet and lava flows are runny, forming gentle slopes around the sides of the volcano.

_____ **60.** The earthquake zone located on the western coast of North America belongs to the zone known as the _____.

Use the skills you have developed in the chapter to answer each question.

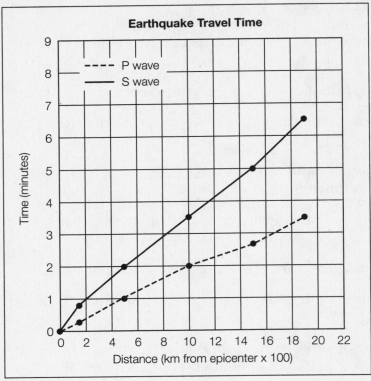

Figure 5

61. How much time did it take for the S wave in Figure 5 to travel a distance of 1200 km?

62. Which earthquake wave in Figure 5 reached a distance of 1750 km first?

63. What was the speed of the P wave in Figure 5 when it reached a distance of 100 km? (*Hint:* Speed is distance divided by time.)

64. In Figure 5, how much faster was the P wave traveling than the S wave when it reached a distance of 500 km?

65. How much time does it take for the S wave in Figure 5 to travel 1000 km?

66. In Figure 5, what is the distance from the epicenter of the earthquake to the seismic recording station?

67. Predict how much time it would take for the P wave in Figure 5 to reach a distance 2200 km away from the epicenter.

68. Based on the curved line produced by the P wave in Figure 5, what can you infer about the speed of that wave?

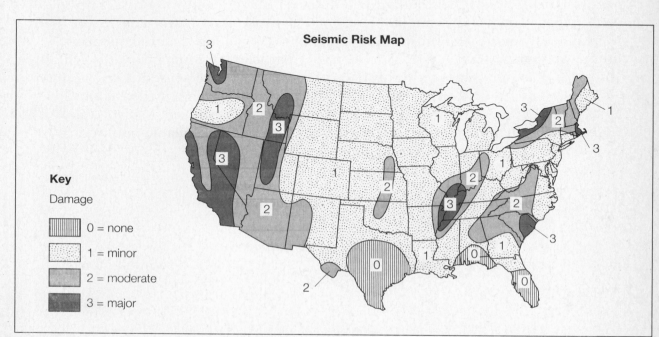

Figure 6

69. According to Figure 6, what part of the United States is least likely to suffer earthquake damage?

70. According to Figure 6, what earthquake damage is Texas likely to suffer?

71. According to Figure 6, how do California and Nevada compare in possible severity of earthquake damage?

72. In Figure 6, what direction does the major earthquake risk zone in Idaho run?

CRITICAL THINKING AND APPLICATION

Discuss each of the following in a brief paragraph.

73. You live on a small island in the Caribbean. Your home is located on a gentle rising hill, 6.5 km from the town of Pugo, which rests on the north shore of the island. One afternoon, you are out in the field gathering hay when a narrow fissure about 20 m long opens in the ground. Thirty minutes later you see smoke coming from the fissure, and within an hour you hear a loud rushing sound of gases coming from the opening. Within two hours hot ash and small molten rock particles are issuing from the vent. By ten o'clock that night, smooth, runny flows of black lava have emerged from the vent and run across your field and down the hill toward Pugo. The lava moved at a steady rate of 10 m per hour down the hill. Pugo is certain to be destroyed. Can you think of at least two things that you and the citizens of Pugo can do with available resources to prevent the lava flow from destroying the town?

74. Create a diagram of L, P, and S seismic waves to illustrate in correct order the events that occur during an earthquake. Identify the L, P, and S waves in your diagram.

75. How would a volcanic eruption under the sea differ from a volcanic eruption on dry land?

76. Suggest a way to distinguish basalt from scoria.

77. How do you account for layers of coral fossils on top of the ridges of an extinct volcano?

78. If you worked as a volcanologist, state at least three tasks that would be included in your job description.

79. Compare and contrast a shield volcano and a composite volcano.

80. Explain the difference between P and S waves in an earthquake.

81. How is the Richter scale used to describe earthquakes?

82. Distinguish between the focus and the epicenter of an earthquake.

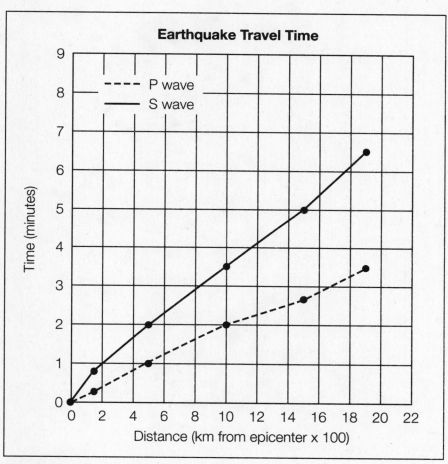

Figure 5

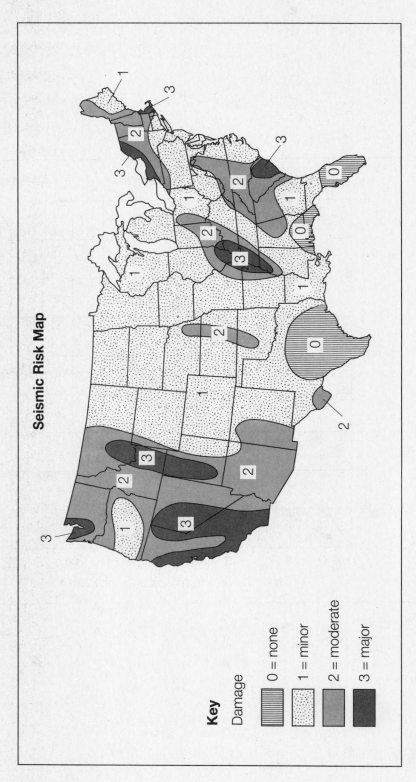

Seismic Risk Map

Key

Damage

0 = none

1 = minor

2 = moderate

3 = major

Figure 6

Test Bank Answer Key

1. c
2. d
3. d
4. c
5. b
6. c
7. d
8. b
9. c
10. a
11. b
12. c
13. b
14. b

15. c
16. b
17. c
18. b
19. d
20. c
21. d
22. c
23. a
24. b
25. a
26. d
27. c
28. d

29. a
30. d
31. F
32. T
33. F
34. F
35. T
36. F
37. T
38. T
39. F
40. F

41. faulting
42. epicenter
43. earthquake
44. Richter
45. focus
46. 3
47. P or primary
48. L or surface
49. seismogram
50. strength
51. magma
52. lava
53. vent
54. dark
55. silica
56. cinder; composite
57. composite
58. crater
59. shield
60. Ring of Fire
61. 4 min
62. P wave
63. 500 km/min
64. 250 km/min faster
65. 3.5 min
66. 1900 km
67. 4 min
68. Speed was rather constant because the curve is essentially a straight line.
69. southern part including Texas, Mississippi, Alabama, and Florida
70. None in the central part of the state. The northern part could suffer minor damage, and a portion of the southwestern part may suffer moderate damage.
71. Both states would suffer moderate to severe damage from an earthquake.
72. north and south

73. Student answers will vary. One solution might be to erect a massive earthen dam to divert the lava flow around the town. Another solution might be to install a strong water pumping system and utilize firefighting equipment to drench the oncoming lava so it will harden and stop.

74. Check student diagrams.

75. An undersea volcano would expel lava that would cool more quickly and not move far from the vent. Rocks would cool more quickly and stay closer together. Tremendous amounts of steam would also be generated.

76. Basalt is dark and very dense. It contains a lot of water and lacks generous gas pockets throughout its entire makeup.

77. The volcano sank below sea level, perhaps due to an earthquake. During that time, corals grew on the slopes of the volcano. At a later time, the volcano was raised above sea level, exposing the fossils.

78. Student answers may vary. Possible answers include: determining the origin of a volcano; identifying the kinds of materials a volcano releases; studying the shape a volcano develops; and studying the changes that occur in volcanic activities.

79. Shield volcanoes are quiet when they form, while composite volcanoes begin violently then continue with alternating quiet and violent eruptions. Shield volcanoes are composed of repeating layers of runny lava, while composite volcanoes are made of alternating layers of lava and rock particles.

80. P waves are push-pull waves, while S waves are not. S waves are not as fast as P waves, and they do not travel through liquids as P waves can.

81. The Richter scale assigns each earthquake a number called its magnitude, which is calculated from the height of the wavy lines recorded by a seismograph and the distance of the seismograph from the epicenter. The magnitude reflects the strength of an earthquake. The higher the number on the scale, the stronger the earthquake. On the Richter scale, an earthquake of 2 is 10 times stronger than an earthquake of 1 and releases about 31 times more energy.

82. The focus is the actual location in the Earth where an earthquake begins, while the epicenter is a point on the Earth's surface directly above the focus of an earthquake.

Contents

CHAPTER 3 ■ Plate Tectonics

Chapter Test

CHAPTER 3 ■ Plate Tectonics

MULTIPLE CHOICE

Write the letter of the correct answer on the line at the left.

_____ 1. Which of the following is an extinct reptile whose fossils provide evidence that South America and Africa were once joined?
   a. *Mesosaurus*
   b. *Glossopteris*
   c. Thecodont
   d. Labyrinthodont

_____ 2. Ocean-floor spreading occurs along
   a. trenches.
   b. midocean ridges.
   c. island areas.
   d. convergent boundaries.

_____ 3. Another name for a destructive boundary is a
   a. convergent boundary.
   b. divergent boundary.
   c. constructive boundary.
   d. transform boundary.

_____ 4. Subduction occurs at
   a. rift valleys.
   b. midocean ridges.
   c. transform boundaries.
   d. trenches.

_____ 5. Strike-slip boundaries occur where two plates
   a. move downward.
   b. move upward.
   c. slide over one another.
   d. slide past one another.

_____ 6. Both plates buckle upward when
   a. two continental plates collide.
   b. two oceanic plates collide.
   c. an oceanic plate collides with a continental plate.
   b. any two plates collide.

_____ 7. Island arcs occur near
   a. divergent boundaries.
   b. constructive boundaries.
   c. destructive boundaries.
   d. strike-slip boundaries.

_____ 8. Which of the following was a giant continent from which all modern continents came?
   a. Laurasia
   b. Gondwanaland
   c. Pangaea
   d. Panthalassa

_____ 9. According to the most widespread hypothesis, the source of the forces that move plates is
   a. magnetism.
   b. gravity.
   c. the Earth's rotation.
   d. convention currents.

_____ 10. The deepest part of the oceans are
   a. midocean ridges.
   b. rift valleys.
   c. divergent boundaries.
   d. trenches.

COMPLETION

Complete each statement on the line at the left.

_____ 1. The name of the scientist who proposed the theory of continental drift is _____.

_____ 2. The topmost solid part of the Earth is called the _____.

_____ 3. A movement of material caused by differences in temperature is called a(an) _____.

_____ 4. Another name for a strike-slip boundary is a lateral _____.

_____ 5. _____ are the moving, irregularly-shaped pieces of lithosphere that fit together to form the surface of the Earth.

TRUE OR FALSE

Determine whether each statement is true or false. If it is true, write T. If it is false, change the underlined word or words to make the statement true.

_____ _____ 1. A deep crack that runs along the center of a midocean ridge is called a rift valley.

_____ _____ 2. The Earth's magnetic poles have reversed themselves in the past.

_____ _____ 3. Trenches are found mostly far from continents.

_____ _____ 4. All plates contain oceanic crust.

_____ _____ 5. Remains or traces of plant or animal life are called fossils.

USING SCIENCE SKILLS: Applying Definitions, Making Comparisons, Relating Concepts, Interpreting Diagrams

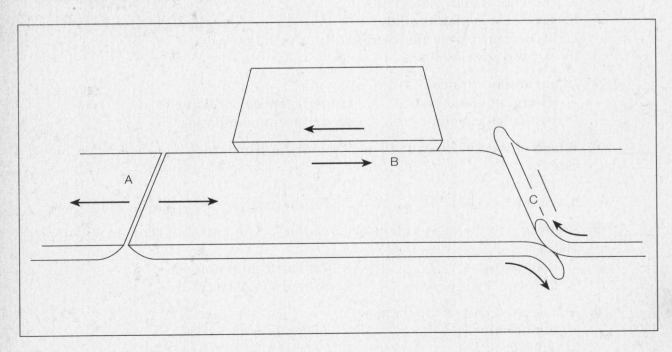

1. What type of plate boundary is A? _____

   B? _____

   C? _____

2. At which boundary is subduction occurring? _____

3. Which boundary is a trench? _____

   Which is a rift valley? _____

   Which is a transform fault? _____

4. At which boundary will midocean ridges tend to form? _____

   Near which boundary will island arcs tend to form? _____

ESSAY

Write a brief paragraph discussing each of the following statements or questions.

1. Discuss one example of evidence of continental drift that was gathered from fossil studies and one example of evidence that was gathered from rock studies.

   _____

   _____

   _____

   _____

   _____

   _____

   _____

   _____

   _____

   _____

   _____

   _____

   _____

2. Contrast what occurs when two oceanic plates collide, when two continental plates

collide, and when an oceanic and a continental plate collide. _____

_____

_____

_____

_____

_____

_____

_____

_____

_____

3. How has the study of magnetic stripes near midocean ridges revealed information about

the Earth's magnetic poles and about the ocean floor? _____

_____

_____

_____

_____

_____

_____

4. Describe the theory of plate tectonics. _____

_____

_____

_____

_____

_____

_____

Answer Key

MULTIPLE CHOICE

1. a 2. b 3. a 4. d 5. d 6. a 7. c 8. c 9. d 10. d

COMPLETION

1. Alfred Wegener 2. lithosphere (Crust is also acceptable.) 3. convection current 4. fault 5. Plates

TRUE OR FALSE

1. T 2. T 3. F, close to 4. T 5. T

USING SCIENCE SKILLS

1. divergent; strike-slip; convergent 2. C 3. C; A; B 4. A; C

ESSAY

1. Answers will vary. Some students will discuss the location of fossils of *Glossopteris* or *Mesosaurus* as fossil-study examples. Some students will discuss the location of mountain ranges, glacial deposits, and salt, coal, and limestone deposits as rock-study examples. 2. When two oceanic plates collide, one is subducted under the other, forming a trench and perhaps resulting in volcanic activity and island-arc formation. When two continental plates collide, the edges of both buckle upward, form-ing large mountain ranges. When an oceanic and a continental plate collide, the former is subduct-ed into a trench, and the latter is pushed up and folded and tends to develop volcanoes. 3. The dif-ferent directions in which molten magnetic mineral particles lined up in different stripes as they solidified revealed that the Earth's magnetic poles, which determine the directions of such lineup, have reversed themselves repeatedly in the past. The matching pattern of magnetic stripes on oppo-site sides of midocean ridges revealed that half the rocks moved away in one direction and half moved away in the other, demonstrating that ocean-floor spreading has occurred. 4. According to the theory of plate tectonics, the lithosphere is made up of a number of plates that contain oceanic and continental crust. Some scientists believe that convection currents within the mantle cause the plates to move. Plate movement explains the formation of the Earth's crust and its movements, colli-sions, and destruction.

Test Bank Test

CHAPTER 3 ■ Plate Tectonics

MULTIPLE CHOICE

Write the letter of the answer that best completes each statement.

_____ **1.** According to the theory of continental drift,
  a. all landmasses on the Earth were originally grouped into two separate continents.
  b. Panthalassa was a continent containing South America and Africa.
  c. the Earth had one original landmass.
  d. Pangaea was submerged beneath the ocean.

_____ **2.** The theory of continental drift was developed by
  a. Isaac Newton.   c. Charles F. Richter.
  b. William F. Fisher.   d. Alfred Wegener.

_____ **3.** Not among evidence to support the theory of continental drift are
  a. ice sheets of the Arctic.   c. *Mesosaurus* fossils.
  b. *Glossopteris* leaf fossils.   d. glacial rock deposits.

_____ **4.** Scientists refused at first to accept the theory of continental drift because
  a. they had no way to match fossils.
  b. rock sediments could not be matched.
  c. they did not believe that continents moved.
  d. they knew that continents could not contain massive faults.

_____ **5.** Michigan has salt deposits hundreds of millions of years old because
  a. glaciers deposited them.
  b. an early freshwater ocean once existed there.
  c. Michigan passed from one climate to another.
  d. erosion left salt deposits.

_____ **6.** Old ocean floor is destroyed, absorbed by the Earth, and remelted beneath
  a. guyots.   c. trenches.
  b. ocean ridges.   d. rift valleys.

_____ **7.** The sea floor is spreading because
  a. the newest rocks are found in trenches.
  b. young rocks are found near ocean ridges.
  c. old rocks are found near the center of ocean ridges.
  d. the youngest rocks are formed in subduction zones.

_____ **8.** Magnetic stripes in ocean floor rocks tell us that
  a. our magnetic poles reversed throughout geologic time.
  b. continental landmasses are stationary.
  c. new rocks form in subduction zones.
  d. Gondwanaland was the first supercontinent on the Earth.

_____ 9. At the mid-ocean ridge, continental plates are
     a. colliding.
     b. separating.
     c. moving over one another.
     d. being destroyed.

_____ 10. The theory of plate tectonics does not help explain
     a. the formation of glacial deposits.
     b. the origin of volcanoes.
     c. earthquakes.
     d. the beginning of mountains.

_____ 11. Most lithospheric plates contain
     a. only continental crust.
     b. oceanic and continental crust.
     c. continental crust attached to molten outer core material.
     d. only oceanic crust.

_____ 12. A major lithospheric plate is the
     a. Caribbean plate.
     b. Arabian plate.
     c. Philippines plate.
     d. African plate.

_____ 13. If a lithospheric plate has subduction zones for a boundary all the way around, it is
     a. increasing in size.
     b. not changing in size.
     c. getting smaller in size.
     d. a constructive plate.

_____ 14. In most cases, the boundaries of lithospheric plates are on
     a. the edges of the continents.
     b. river channels.
     c. shorelines.
     d. the ocean floor.

_____ 15. The city of Los Angeles is located on the
     a. Caribbean plate.
     b. Cocos plate.
     c. North American plate.
     d. Pacific plate.

_____ 16. Plates in strike-slip boundaries
     a. remain stationary.
     b. are under tension and being pulled apart.
     c. horizontally slide past each other.
     d. result in a thrust fault.

_____ 17. When two continental plates collide,
     a. they are pushed down into the mantle.
     b. they buckle upward and form mountains.
     c. they remain level since densities in both plates are equal.
     d. one plate overrides the other and forms a trench.

_____ 18. Scientists believe that the lithosperic plates of the Earth move because
     a. a fault separates each plate from the mantle below.
     b. volcanic activity on one end of the plate pushes the plate in the opposite direction.
     c. the spin of the Earth forces the plates to move in the direction the Earth is rotating.
     d. crustal plates slide along with the circular movement of molten magma in the mantle.

_____ 19. Continental crust is different from oceanic crust because it
     a. is composed of less dense materials.
     b. floats on mantle materials below.
     c. is made of igneous rock.
     d. is thinner.

_____ **20.** At a point where a dense oceanic plate and light continental plate collide,
     a. the continental plate slides under the oceanic plate.
     b. mountains develop on the oceanic plate.
     c. the oceanic plate is forced down under the continental plate.
     d. neither plate drops down into the mantle.

_____ **21.** When two oceanic plates collide,
     a. they push upward to form mountains.
     b. one plate is subducted under the other and forms a trench.
     c. they fuse together and form a flat plain.
     d. both plates are pushed down into the mantle.

_____ **22.** As two oceanic plates separate at their joint boundary,
     a. one plate is drawn under the second plate.
     b. the mantle reclaims both plates.
     c. a ridge develops.
     d. many active volcanoes develop at the boundary.

_____ **23.** Oceanic plate material is absorbed back into the mantle at
     a. ocean ridges.   c. divergent boundaries.
     b. ocean trenches.   d. constructive boundaries.

_____ **24.** In order to find the deepest parts of the ocean, you would look for
     a. rift valleys.   c. guyots.
     b. ocean ridges.   d. trenches.

_____ **25.** Which of the following is an extinct seed fern?
     a. *Glossopteris*   c. Thecodont
     b. *Mesosaurus*   d. Labyrinthodont

_____ **26.** The formations that run down the centers of midocean ridges are called
     a. destructive boundaries.   c. island arcs.
     b. trenches.   d. rift valleys.

_____ **27.** The process in which ocean floor returns to the Earth's interior is called
     a. subduction.   c. construction.
     b. divergence.   d. ocean floor spreading.

_____ **28.** Compared to the oldest rocks on the ocean floor, the oldest rocks on land are
     a. younger.   c. slightly older.
     b. the same age.   d. much older.

_____ **29.** Most of the molten rock produced during subduction
     a. becomes part of the crust.   c. becomes part of the mantle.
     b. becomes part of the core.   d. rises up and produces volcanoes.

_____ **30.** The lithosphere
     a. is the solid topmost part of the Earth.
     b. is the same as the mantle.
     c. includes the ocean floor but not the continents.
     d. includes the continents but not the ocean floor.

TRUE OR FALSE

Determine whether each statement is true or false.

_____ 31. Fossils are used to support the idea that continents were once joined together.

_____ 32. Fossils are formed only from the remains of animal life preserved in rock.

_____ 33. Fossils of *Mesosaurus* have been discovered in both Africa and South America.

_____ 34. Scientists agree that *Glossopteris* seeds drifted from one continent to another and thus cannot be used as direct evidence of continental drift.

_____ 35. The midocean ridges form the single largest mountain chain in the world.

_____ 36. Ocean floor spreading is a concept that has no connection with the theory of continental drift.

_____ 37. The lithosphere is composed of eleven major plates.

_____ 38. Divergent boundaries are sites of new crustal formation.

_____ 39. All lithospheric plates move at the same speed and in the same direction.

_____ 40. The topmost solid part of the Earth is called the hydrosphere.

COMPLETION

Fill in the word or number that best completes each statement.

_____ 41. The German scientist Alfred Wegener proposed that all land on Earth was joined into a supercontinent called _____.

_____ 42. The idea suggested by Alfred Wegener that the Earth's continents drifted to their present locations is called _____.

_____ 43. A deep crack called the _____ runs through the center of the midocean ridge.

_____ 44. The process of _____ involves crust of the Earth being returned back into the mantle of the Earth.

_____ 45. Deep V-shaped valleys known as _____ are located near the edges of continents where ocean floor plunges back into the Earth's interior.

_____ 46. The movements of the Earth's crust are studied in a special branch of Earth science known as _____.

_____ 47. The largest of all our lithospheric plates is the _____ plate.

_____ 48. Lithospheric plates are composed of both continental and _____ crustal materials.

_____ 49. Most of the lithospheric plate boundaries are located on the _____ floor.

_____ 50. Many scientists believe that lithospheric plates are moved across the surface of the Earth by _____ currents within the Earth.

_____ **51.** At plate boundaries where subduction occurs, denser _____ plates slide under continental plates and are remelted in the mantle of the Earth.

_____ **52.** As two continental plates contact each other, neither returns to the Earth's mantle because their _____ is nearly the same.

_____ **53.** The San Andreas fault in California is an example of a _____ boundary.

_____ **54.** When two oceanic plates collide, a deep _____ is formed at the zone where they make contact.

_____ **55.** _____ are the preserved remains of ancient organisms.

_____ **56.** Underwater mountain chains that form plate boundaries are called _____.

_____ **57.** _____ spreading helps to explain how continents drift.

_____ **58.** The topmost solid part of the Earth is called the _____.

_____ **59.** _____ boundaries are places where plates move apart.

_____ **60.** _____ boundaries are places where plates come together.

USING SCIENCE SKILLS

Use the skills you have developed in the chapter to answer each question.

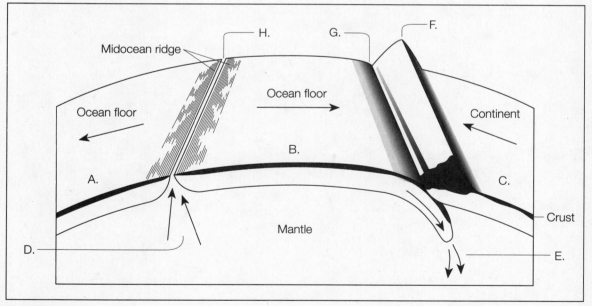

Figure 7

61. What does the diagram in Figure 7 illustrate?

62. What is happening at point E in Figure 7?

63. With respect to each other, what activities are occurring between plates A and B in Figure 7?

64. What feature is forming at point G in Figure 7? Why is it forming?

65. In Figure 7, why is feature F forming on the border of continental plate C?

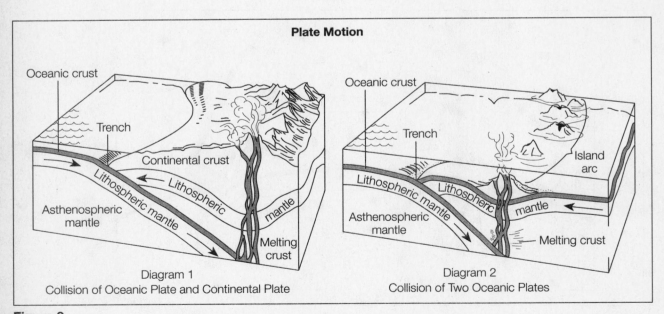

Figure 8

66. Which of the two plates in diagram 1 of Figure 8 is the thickest? Why?

67. Is the plate boundary shown in diagram 2 of Figure 8 a convergent or a divergent boundary? Explain.

68. Why does an island arc form in diagram 2 and not in diagram 1 of Figure 8?

69. How are diagrams 1 and 2 in Figure 8 alike? Different?

70. Will a rift valley develop and form new crust in diagram 2 of Figure 8? Explain.

71. Why does melting crust develop in just about the same place in diagrams 1 and 2 of Figure 8?

CRITICAL THINKING AND APPLICATION

Discuss each of the following in a brief paragraph.

72. If new ocean floor is being made continually in the ocean ridge zones, why isn't the Earth growing in size?

73. Were Africa and South America ever joined? Cite geological evidence to support your answer.

74. How does magnetic striping of the ocean floor serve as a form of recorded history of our planet?

75. The Eurasian and North American continental plates share a common border. If the Eurasian plate moves east and the North American plate moves west, explain what plate activity occurs at their common boundary.

76. The Pacific plate, which includes Los Angeles, is moving 4 cm per year to the northwest along the California coast. Los Angeles is 611 km from San Francisco, which is not moving northwest. How long will it take for Los Angeles to reach San Francisco?

77. Study the map in Figure 9. The light-outlined areas represent the continents today, and the dark-outlined areas represent continental crust in the past. Interpret what happened to continental landmass B over time.

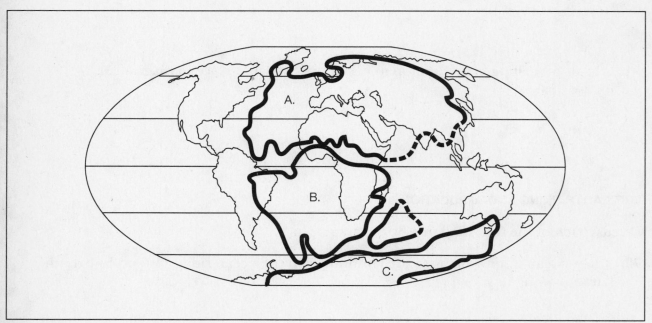

Figure 9

78. Draw a diagram to illustrate the collision of oceanic crust and continental crust. In the diagram show, by means of arrows, the role that convection currents in the Earth may play in this process, and label the oceanic crust, continental crust, and convection currents.

79. If it takes approximately 750,000 years to form each strip of new ocean floor in Figure 10, how many years ago would strip E have formed?

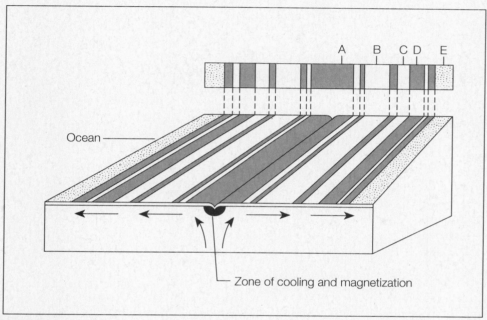

Zone of cooling and magnetization

Figure 10

80. Your school building is moving with the North American plate. What will be the location of your school building 1 million years from today? *(Hint:* The North American plate is moving 3 cm west each year.)

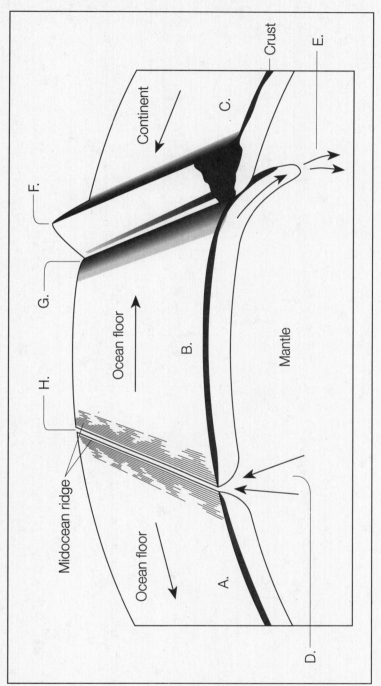

Figure 7

Plate Motion

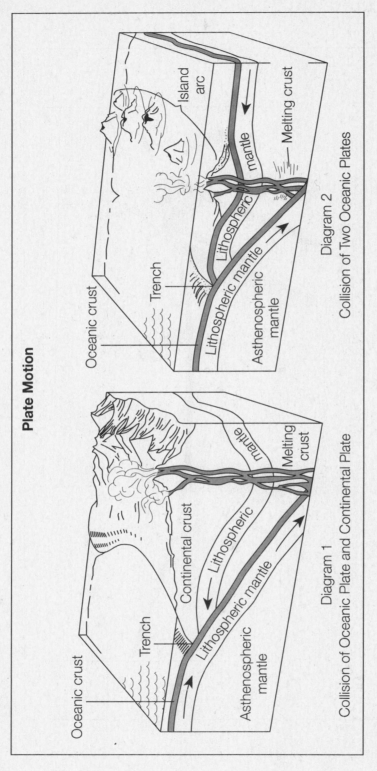

Oceanic crust

Trench

Continental crust

Lithospheric
mantle

Asthenospheric
mantle

Lithospheric mantle

mantle

Melting
crust

Diagram 1
Collision of Oceanic Plate and Continental Plate

Oceanic crust

Trench

Island
arc

Lithospheric
mantle

Lithospheric mantle

Asthenospheric
mantle

Melting crust

Diagram 2
Collision of Two Oceanic Plates

Figure 8

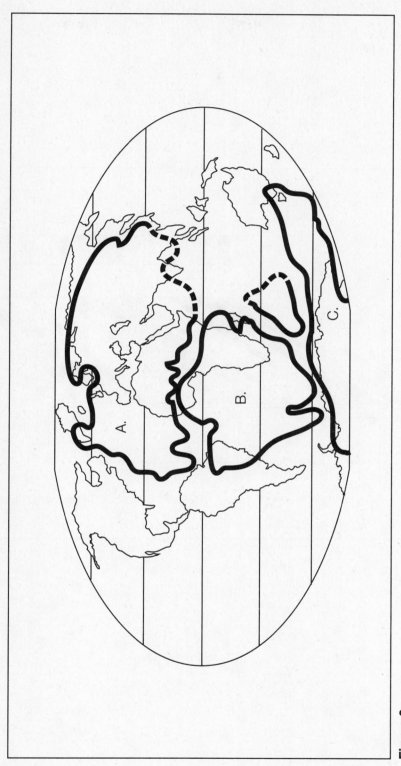

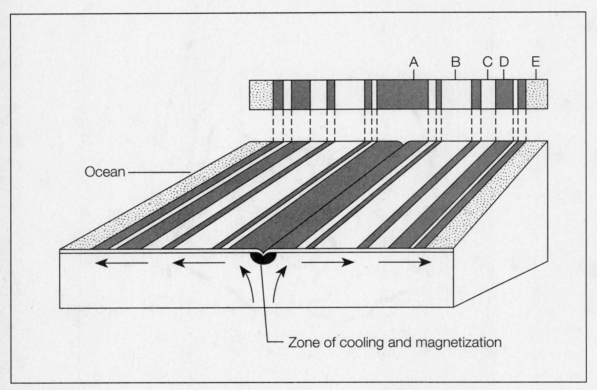

Figure 10

Test Bank Answer Key

1. c	15. d	29. c
2. d	16. c	30. a
3. d	17. b	31. T
4. c	18. d	32. F
5. c	19. a	33. T
6. c	20. c	34. F
7. b	21. b	35. T
8. a	22. c	36. F
9. b	23. b	37. F
10. a	24. d	38. T
11. b	25. a	39. F
12. d	26. d	40. F
13. c	27. a	
14. d	28. d	

41. Pangaea
42. continental drift
43. rift valley
44. subduction
45. trenches
46. tectonics
47. Pacific
48. oceanic
49. ocean
50. convection
51. oceanic
52. density
53. strike-slip or conservative
54. trench
55. Fossils
56. midocean ridges
57. Ocean-floor
58. lithosphere
59. divergent or constructive
60. convergent or destructive
61. The diagram in Figure 7 shows the ocean floor spreading and being destroyed.
62. The leading edge of the ocean floor is being pushed under the continental plate and is being remelted by the mantle.
63. The two plates are pulled apart because each plate is moving in the opposite direction. New ocean floor is formed in the opening created by the movement of the two plates.
64. The feature being formed is a trench. It forms because, as the two plates collide, the lighter continental plate rides over the more dense oceanic plate. The trench forms where the oceanic plate is pushed down.
65. Feature F, a mountain range, is forming because the border of the plate is being pushed up by the oceanic plate, forming a folded mountain chain.
66. The continental plate is thickest because the collision between the two plates causes the continental plate to be pushed up. Also, continental plate material is less dense than oceanic plate material.
67. The boundary is a convergent boundary because the motion, indicated by the arrows in each plate, indicates that the two plates are being pushed together.

68. The subducted plate breaks through the other plate as active volcanoes in the sea. As the volcanoes cool and harden, they form islands. No islands form in diagram 1 because the continental plate is not covered by the sea.

69. The two diagrams are alike because plate collisions take place in both. They are different because diagram 1 shows an oceanic plate and a continental plate colliding, while diagram 2 shows two oceanic plates colliding.

70. No rift valley will form because the two plates are colliding. Rift valleys form where two plates are moving apart and new sea floor is set in place.

71. Melting crust develops in just about the same place because old crust is returned to the hot mantle area below, causing the solid rock to melt when heated.

72. As the ocean floor spreads and forms new crust, there are other crustal areas on the Earth's surface that are being subducted back into the mantle of the Earth and remelted. These two activities balance each other and the Earth does not grow in size.

73. Fossils of the extinct freshwater *Mesosaurus* have been found both in Africa and South America. They could not have swum across the Atlantic Ocean. Also, extinct *Glossopteris* leaves have been found in both Africa and South America. In addition, folded mountain patterns in Africa fit well with those found in South America, suggesting that the two landmasses were once united.

74. As new ocean floor forms in midocean ridges, some of that rock is magnetic and will align itself with the present North Pole and harden in that position. As time elapses, the poles of the Earth naturally reverse themselves. As new rock forms again at the midocean ridge, the new magnetic rock aligns itself with the North Pole in a reversed direction. This reverse alignment of polarity in rock beds over long periods of time provides a permanent history of the early Earth.

75. The common boundary would undergo a splitting or divergence. This would cause the area to split and allow new molten rock to come to the surface and harden. Since this would occur in the ocean, a midocean ridge would form at the boundary.

76. 15,275,000 years

Solution: Convert kilometers to centimeters:

611 km × 1000 m = 611,000 m
611,000 m × 100 cm = 61,100,000 cm

Find out how many years it will take:

61,100,000 cm / 4 cm = 15,275,000 years

77. Landmass B seems to have split into two landmasses. One drifted northwest to form South America, and the other drifted northeast to form Africa.

78.

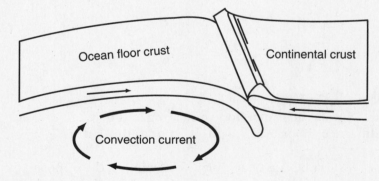

79. 3,750,000 years (5 × 750,000 yrs.)

80. 30 km west of where it is right now.

Solution: If the plate is moving an average of 3 cm per year, then:

3 cm × 1,000,000 years = 3,000,000 cm
3,000,000 cm / 100 cm = 30,000 m = 30 km

Since the plate is moving west, the new location would be west of the present location.

Contents

CHAPTER 4 ■ Rocks and Minerals

Chapter Test

CHAPTER 4 ■ Rocks and Minerals

MULTIPLE CHOICE

Write the letter of the correct answer on the line at the left.

_____ **1.** Which of the following describes minerals?
    a. liquid.   c. synthetic
    b. organic   d. definite composition

_____ **2.** The luster of a mineral describes
    a. the way it reflects light.   c. its ability to resist being scratched.
    b. its color.   d. its density.

_____ **3.** Rubbing a mineral sample across unglazed ceramic is the usual way of determining
    a. streak.   c. hardness.
    b. luster.   d. density.

_____ **4.** Which of the following is a nonmetallic mineral?
    a. sulfur   c. aluminum
    b. lead   d. copper

_____ **5.** Rocks that form when great heat, pressure, and chemical reactions change existing rocks are called
    a. sedimentary rocks.   c. igneous rocks.
    b. metamorphic rocks.   d. mudrocks.

_____ **6.** Rocks formed from magma are called
    a. sedimentary rocks.   c. clastic rocks.
    b. metamorphic rocks.   d. igneous rocks.

_____ **7.** The size of crystals depends mainly on
    a. pressure.   c. cooling rate.
    b. the presence of water.   d. the presence of air.

_____ **8.** Extrusive rocks are formed
    a. in water.   c. from other rocks.
    b. deep within the Earth.   d. at the Earth's surface.

_____ **9.** Which of the following is an example of a sedimentary rock?
    a. chalk   c. granite
    b. marble   d. obsidian

_____ **10.** Which of the following is an example of a metamorphic rock?
    a. chalk   c. granite
    b. marble   d. obsidian

COMPLETION

Complete each statement on the line at the left.

_____ 1. A mineral or rock from which metals and nonmetals can be removed in usable amounts is called a(an) _____.

_____ 2. The 1 to 10 hardness scale in which the number 1 is assigned to talc is called the _____.

_____ 3. The breaking of a mineral along smooth, definite surfaces is called _____.

_____ 4. Small pieces of rocks, shells, or plant or animal remains carried and deposited by wind, water, and ice are called _____.

_____ 5. Naturally occurring solids made of minerals are _____.

TRUE OR FALSE

Determine whether each statement is true or false. If it is true, write T. If it is false, change the underlined word or words to make the statement true.

_____ _____ 1. When magma cools rapidly, large crystals form.

_____ _____ 2. A mineral with a hardness of 6 will scratch a mineral with a hardness of more than 6.

_____ _____ 3. The changing of one rock type into another as a result of heat, pressure, and chemical reactions is sedimentation.

_____ _____ 4. Rocks formed directly or indirectly from once-living material are called organic rocks.

_____ _____ 5. The continuous changing of rocks from one type to another is called the rock cycle.

USING SCIENCE SKILLS: Making Comparisons, Identifying Relationships

Mineral	Hardness
Talc	1
Gypsum	2
Calcite	3
Fluorite	4
Apatite	5
Feldspars	6
Quartz	7
Topaz	8
Corundum	9
Diamond	10

1. Which mineral is the hardest? _____

What does this mean? _____

_____

2. What would happen if a piece of fluorite were rubbed against a piece of feldspar?

_____

_____

3. What would you expect to happen if a mineral of hardness 7.5 were rubbed against a

piece of quartz? _____

Against a piece of topaz?_____

4. An unknown mineral is found to scratch apatite and to be scratched by corundum.

What can be said of this mineral's hardness?_____

_____

What experiment might you do to get more information on its hardness?_____

_____

_____

ESSAY

Write a brief paragraph discussing each of the following statements or questions.

1. Describe the five properties all minerals must have. Use this definition to explain why coal, pearls, and synthetic diamonds are not considered minerals.

_____

_____

_____

_____

_____

2. State and define five physical properties other than color used to identify minerals.

_____

_____

_____

_____

_____

3. What are the properties of metallic and nonmetallic minerals? Give two examples of

metallic minerals and two examples of nonmetallic minerals. _____

_____

_____

_____

_____

4. Compare and contrast the formation of coarse-grained and fine-grained igneous rock.

Give an example of each. _____

_____

_____

_____

_____

5. Describe the formation of the three types of sedimentary rocks.

_____

_____

_____

_____

_____

Answer Key

MULTIPLE CHOICE

1. d **2.** a **3.** a **4.** a **5.** b **6.** d **7.** c **8.** d **9.** a **10.** b

COMPLETION

1. ore **2.** Mohs hardness scale **3.** cleavage **4.** oxygen and silicon **5.** rocks

TRUE OR FALSE

1. F, small **2.** F, less **3.** F, metamorphism **4.** T **5.** T

USING SCIENCE SKILLS

1. diamond. It scratches all the others. **2.** The fluorite would be scratched, but not the feldspar. **3.** It would scratch the quartz. It would be scratched by the topaz. **4.** Its hardness is greater than 5 but less than 9. One might try scratching it with feldspar, quartz, and topaz.

ESSAY

1. Minerals must be naturally occurring, solid, and inorganic, and must have definite chemical composition and crystal shape. Coal and pearls are formed from living things, and synthetic diamonds are manufactured. **2.** Luster describes the way in which a mineral reflects light from its surface. Hardness is the ability of a mineral to resist being scratched. Streak is the color of the powder left by a mineral when rubbed against a hard, rough surface. Density is mass per unit volume. Crystal shape is the geometric form the patterns of atoms or molecules in a mineral produce. Cleavage or fracture is the way a mineral breaks. Cleavage is the breakage along smooth, definite surfaces. Fracture is uneven breakage. Other properties include magnetic property, taste, and ability to glow under ultraviolet light. **3.** Metals are malleable, ductile, shiny, and good conductors of heat and electricity. Nonmetals are not malleable, ductile, shiny, or good conductors of heat and electricity. Examples of metallic minerals are gold, silver, copper, iron, and lead. Examples of nonmetallic minerals are sulfur, fluorite, and halite. **4.** Igneous rocks form from cooling magma. Coarse-grained igneous rocks form when the cooling rate is slow, allowing large crystals to form. Coarse-grained igneous rocks are intrusive. Fine-grained igneous rocks form when the cooling rate is fast, allowing only small crystals to form. Fine-grained igneous rocks are usually extrusive. Granite, diorite, gabbro, and peridotite are examples of coarse-grained igneous rocks. Rhyolite, andesite, pumice, and basalt are examples of fine-grained igneous rocks. **5.** Clastic rocks are formed by the compaction and cementation of sediments. Organic rocks are formed directly or indirectly from material that was once living. Chemical rocks are formed by evaporation or inorganic chemical reactions.

Test Bank Test

CHAPTER 4 ■ Rocks and Minerals

MULTIPLE CHOICE

Write the letter of the answer that best completes each statement.

_____ **1.** A mineral that is an example of a precious stone is
   a. emerald.   c. amethyst.
   b. opal.   d. garnet.

_____ **2.** Not all precious stones are
   a. valuable.   c. rare.
   b. beautiful.   d. colorless.

_____ **3.** A mineral that is classified as a metal is
   a. sulfur.   c. copper.
   b. halite.   d. asbestos.

_____ **4.** Which of the following is not a use for aluminum?
   a. production of cans   c. cooking foil
   b. manufacture of airplanes   d. fillings for teeth

_____ **5.** Sulfur is not used to make
   a. medicines.   c. aluminum.
   b. matches.   d. fertilizers.

_____ **6.** Smelting is a process that
   a. extracts gemstones from a mine.
   b. classifies minerals according to hardness.
   c. separates a metal from an ore.
   d. determines crystal shape in naturally occurring minerals.

_____ **7.** An ore mined to obtain iron for use in steel manufacturing is
   a. limonite.   c. galena.
   b. bauxite.   d. corundum.

_____ **8.** Cleavage is the property of a mineral that
   a. permits fizzing when hydrochloric acid is added to its surface.
   b. produces a colored powder line when rubbed on a rough surface.
   c. permits it to be scratched by another mineral.
   d. allows it to break along smooth, definite lines.

_____ **9.** The special property of magnetite is
   a. its ability to leave a powder line when rubbed on a rough surface.
   b. its attraction for certain metals.
   c. its clarity and brilliance as a gemstone.
   d. that it is one of only a few minerals that exhibit color.

_____ 10. Which of the following substances is not a mineral?
   a. silver   c. cement
   b. tourmaline   d. gold

_____ 11. Which of the following substances cannot be classified as a mineral?
   a. beryl   c. talc
   b. diamond   d. coal

_____ 12. The Mohs hardness scale mineral that can scratch gypsum and talc but cannot
         scratch fluorite is
   a. topaz.   c. calcite.
   b. apatite.   d. quartz.

_____ 13. Feldspars will scratch apatite but will not scratch
   a. topaz.   c. gypsum.
   b. fluorite.   d. talc.

_____ 14. According to the Mohs hardness scale, the hardest of the following minerals is
   a. topaz.   c. corundum.
   b. apatite.   d. diamond.

_____ 15. A pearly luster can typically be observed on the mineral
   a. talc.   c. diamond.
   b. quartz.   d. sulfur.

_____ 16. Streak would not be useful in identifying
   a. galena.   c. apatite.
   b. quartz.   d. fluorite.

_____ 17. A streak plate would not be useful in identifying minerals with a hardness of
   a. 8 or 9.   c. 1 or 2.
   b. 5.   d. 3 or 4.

_____ 18. The luster of diamond is usually described as
   a. metallic.   c. dull.
   b. silky.   d. brilliant.

_____ 19. All rocks are classified on the basis of
   a. the elements they contain.   c. where they are found.
   b. the way they are formed.   d. the layers present.

_____ 20. A rock formed from molten rock is
   a. obsidian.   c. gypsum.
   b. conglomerate.   d. shale.

_____ 21. The texture of igneous rocks depends on
   a. cooling the rocks on the surface of the Earth.
   b. trapped gases contained in the rocks.
   c. the time it takes for the rocks to harden.
   d. the conglomerate particles present.

_____ 22. Coarse-grained igneous rocks result when
   a. sedimentary grains are compacted and cemented into a unit.
   b. magma cools very slowly.
   c. large conglomerate particles become cemented together.
   d. hot melted rock undergoes almost instantaneous cooling.

_____ **23.** All intrusive igneous rocks form
   a. deep within the Earth.   c. on the surface of the Earth.
   b. without any crystals present.   d. with crystals less than 1 cm in size.

_____ **24.** Igneous rocks are classified by chemical composition and
   a. luster.   c. streak.
   b. texture.   d. hardness.

_____ **25.** The basic difference between igneous rock and sedimentary rock is
   a. sedimentary rock is made of one mineral.
   b. igneous rock always has small crystals present.
   c. sedimentary rock forms without intense heat being present.
   d. igneous rock has distinctly clear layers present, with the oldest on bottom and youngest on top.

_____ **26.** Fine-grained igneous rocks have
   a. medium crystals.   c. large crystals.
   b. no crystals.   d. small crystals.

_____ **27.** Rocks that are organic and composed of the fragmented remains of ocean animals are probably forms of
   a. gypsum.   c. limestone.
   b. mica.   d. slate.

_____ **28.** The difference between limestone and chalk is that
   a. limestone is a sedimentary rock.
   b. chalk is soft.
   c. limestone contains the remains of ocean animals.
   d. chalk is an organic rock.

_____ **29.** Ripple marks and mud cracks are characteristics of
   a. foliated rocks.   c. metamorphic rocks.
   b. igneous rocks.   d. sedimentary rocks.

_____ **30.** A good example of a coarse-grained igneous rock is
   a. obsidian.   c. basalt.
   b. granite.   d. pumice.

TRUE OR FALSE

Determine whether each statement is true or false.

_____ **31.** A pearl is classified as a mineral because it is made of calcium carbonate.

_____ **32.** A mineral has a definite chemical composition, unique crystal shape, and is of organic origin.

_____ **33.** Mineral crystals may take any one of six basic shapes.

_____ **34.** Obsidian is a black, glassy mineral formed from molten rock.

_____ 35. Hardness is a test that identifies the color of the powder of a mineral when it is rubbed on a rough surface.

_____ 36. Cleavage occurs when a mineral breaks unevenly, leaving a sharp, jagged surface.

_____ 37. The cooling and hardening of hot liquid rock forms igneous rock.

_____ 38. When igneous rocks cool rapidly near the Earth's surface, the crystals that develop in the rock will be small.

_____ 39. Rocks that form from broken pieces or fragments are organic rocks.

_____ 40. Chemical rocks may be formed when water evaporates and leaves behind mineral deposits.

COMPLETION

Fill in the word or number that best completes each statement.

_____ 41. Large crystals form in rock when _____ cools slowly beneath the Earth's crust.

_____ 42. The mineral malachite will always appear _____ in color.

_____ 43. An inorganic, naturally-occurring solid that has a definite chemical composition and crystal shape is known as a(an) _____.

_____ 44. A mineral's _____ is the way the substance reflects light from its surface.

_____ 45. _____ is the hardest mineral in the Mohs hardness scale.

_____ 46. When a mineral is rubbed against a hard, rough surface, it leaves a characteristic _____, showing the color of the powder of the mineral.

_____ 47. A mineral's ability to resist being scratched is its _____.

_____ 48. As they form, all minerals arrange their atoms into _____, which are in a definite pattern repeated over and over again.

_____ 49. The number _____ is the highest number in the Mohs hardness scale.

_____ 50. _____ is the only mineral in the Mohs hardness scale that is scratched by all other minerals in the scale.

_____ 51. _____ occurs when a mineral breaks along a smooth, definite surface.

_____ 52. When quartz breaks, or _____, the result looks like pieces of broken glass.

_____ 53. Rock deposits from which metals and nonmetals can be removed are known as _____.

_____ 54. The most valuable and rarest gemstones that come from the Earth are called _____.

_____ 55. A naturally-formed solid material that is made of one or more minerals or minerallike substances is called a(an) _____.

Name _____ Class _____ Date _____

_____ **56.** Rocks formed by the cooling and hardening of hot liquid rock are classified as _____ rocks.

_____ **57.** When existing rock is changed within the Earth by extreme heat and pressure, the resulting rock is identified as _____ rock.

_____ **58.** Igneous rocks can be further subdivided into two groups known as _____ and _____ igneous rocks.

_____

_____ **59.** Deposits of _____ rock form when loose sediments are pressed and cemented together.

_____ **60.** A(An) _____ rock is made of substances that were once part of or made by living things.

USING SCIENCE SKILLS

Use the skills you have developed in the chapter to answer each question.

Mohs Hardness Scale			
Mineral	Hardness	Streak	Cleavage
Talc	1	White	One direction
Gypsum	2	Clear	One direction
Calcite	3	Clear	Rhombohedral
Fluorite	4	Clear	Octahedral
Apatite	5	White	One direction
Feldspars	6	White or Clear	Two planes
Quartz	7	Clear	None
Topaz	8	Clear	One direction
Corundum	9	Clear	Rhombohedral
Diamond	10	Clear	Octahedral

Figure 11

61. Which minerals in Figure 11 will scratch quartz?

62. Using Figure 11, how would fluorite respond if you scratched it with bornite, which has a hardness of 3?

63. Place arrows in the left margin of Figure 11 to indicate the direction of decreasing hardness on the Mohs scale.

64. Using Figure 11, predict what the hardness of chlorite is if its hardness lies between the hardness of gypsum and calcite.

65. Use Figure 11 to describe the hardness, streak, and cleavage of feldspars.

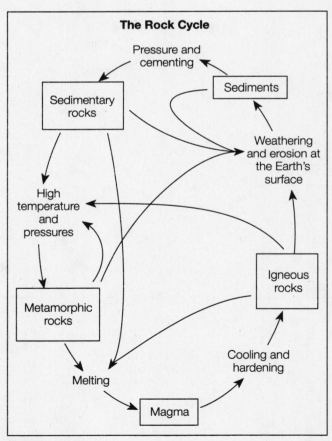

Figure 12

66. Using Figure 12, explain what happens to magma once it cools and hardens.

67. Using the information given in Figure 12, decide whether metamorphic rock is the only type of rock that serves as a source of material for making magma. Explain.

68. From the information given in Figure 12, must sedimentary rock become metamorphic rock before it can be turned back into magma? Explain.

69. Using Figure 12, state two ways in which igneous rock can become metamorphic rock. Include the processes that the igneous rock must undergo.

70. Based on information in Figure 12, how does the conversion of sediments into rock differ from the conversion of sedimentary rock into metamorphic rock?

CRITICAL THINKING AND APPLICATION

Discuss each of the following in a brief paragraph.

71. Why it is very difficult to identify a mineral by its color?

72. Describe the process you would follow in determining the hardness of a mineral sample you have never seen before.

73. Design an experiment that would allow you to confirm which minerals in a group of unknown minerals will conduct electricity. Make sure you test only one variable (conductance of electricity) in the experiment.

74. You win a ring containing a one-half-carat "diamond" at a drawing held during an anniversary celebration at a famous department store. You pick up your prize and return home. Besides taking the ring to a jeweler, how else could you test the stone to see if it is really a diamond?

75. The surface of the Earth is composed of minerals and rocks. Many manufactured products are being made from these materials. Why do we need to be concerned about the conservation of mineral resources?

76. There are three basic types of rocks that can be studied in the field. They are igneous, sedimentary, and metamorphic rocks. You have learned that excellent fossils can be collected from one of these rock types. Which rock type is this? Explain. State reasons you would not want to look for fossils in the other two rock types.

77. Describe a sequence of events in the rock cycle that would cause magma eventually to form sedimentary rock.

78. How does a rock differ from a mineral?

79. Describe at least three ways rocks are useful to people in everyday life.

80. Explain why metamorphic rocks rarely form at the surface of the Earth.

Mohs Hardness Scale

Mineral	Hardness	Streak	Cleavage
Talc	1	White	One direction
Gypsum	2	Clear	One direction
Calcite	3	Clear	Rhombohedral
Fluorite	4	Clear	Octahedral
Apatite	5	White	One direction
Feldspars	6	White or Clear	Two planes
Quartz	7	Clear	None
Topaz	8	Clear	One direction
Corundum	9	Clear	Rhombohedral
Diamond	10	Clear	Octahedral

Figure 11

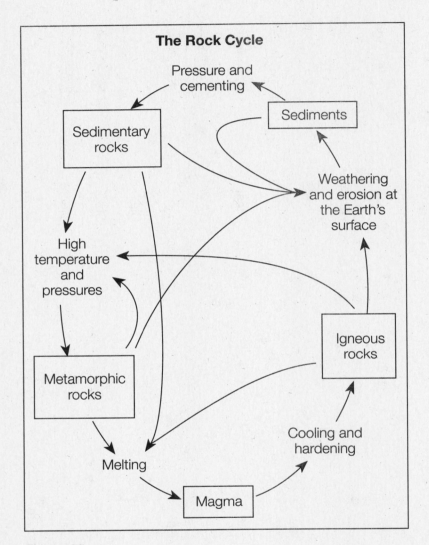

Figure 12

Test Bank Answer Key

1. a
2. d
3. c
4. d
5. c
6. c
7. a
8. d
9. b
10. c
11. d
12. c
13. b
14. d

15. a
16. b
17. a
18. b
19. b
20. a
21. c
22. b
23. a
24. b
25. c
26. d
27. c
28. b

29. d
30. b
31. F
32. F
33. T
34. F
35. F
36. F
37. T
38. T
39. F
40. T

41. magma
42. green
43. mineral
44. luster
45. Diamond
46. streak
47. hardness
48. crystals
49. 10
50. Talc
51. Cleavage
52. fractures
53. ores
54. precious stones
55. rock
56. igneous
57. metamorphic
58. intrusive, extrusive
59. sedimentary (Clastic is also acceptable.)
60. organic
61. topaz, corundum, diamond
62. It would not be scratched by bornite.
63. Figure 11 should have an arrow in the left margin pointing from the bottom of the chart to the top of the chart.
64. hardness approximately 2.5
65. Feldspars have a hardness of 6, a white or clear streak, and two-planed cleavage.
66. The magma turns into igneous rock.
67. No. Igneous and sedimentary rock can also serve as sources.
68. No. Sedimentary and igneous rocks can undergo intense heating and be remelted into magma without ever becoming metamorphic rock.
69. First, igneous rock can undergo high temperature and pressure and turn into metamorphic rock directly. Second, igneous rock can undergo weathering and erosion to form sedimentary rock, which in turn undergoes high temperature and pressure to become metamorphic rock.

70. The sedimentary rock formation process requires cementing, while the metamorphic rock formation process requires high temperatures.

71. Color is very easy to observe, but there are only a few minerals that always have a particular color. Many minerals come in a variety of colors, and the color on most minerals changes as the mineral remains exposed to air, rain, and other conditions that occur in nature.

72. The hardness can be determined by using common objects of known hardness or by using a Mohs hardness mineral set. First, take the sample and scratch it against the softest known object or mineral. If the sample leaves a scratch on the object or mineral of known hardness, scratch the unknown mineral against an object or mineral of the next higher known hardness. Continue this process until the unknown mineral no longer scratches objects or minerals of known hardness. At that point, the unknown mineral is at the same hardness and it will be scratched by the object or mineral of the next higher hardness.

73. First, make a simple direct current, low voltage circuit with a small bulb. See example in answer key. (A hand-held DC volt-ohm meter will also work.)

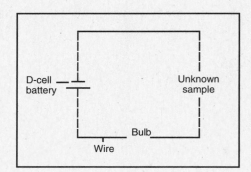

Test your circuit to make sure that electricity will flow through it. If you use the bulb circuit, the bulb should light. If you use the meter, the needle on the dial should move. Take one unknown sample and touch each wire of the test circuit to opposite sides of the sample. Observe the bulb (meter). If it lights or moves, the mineral conducts electricity. Record your answer on a data table for specimen 1. Repeat the same test on the remaining nine minerals, recording your test results. When you have finished, group those that conduct electricity in one group and those that do not in another group. If you are not sure about any of the results, rerun the tests. After you finish, state a conclusion.

74. Possible answer: Use a piece of corundum from a Mohs hardness set and see if the corundum will scratch the "diamond." If not, the stone in the ring is harder than corundum. Also check to see if the stone in the ring will scratch the corundum. If it does, the stone is harder than the corundum.

75. The mineral resources we use up are not replaced and thus are nonrenewable resources. We have continually exploited and utilized easy-to-get sources, thus many of those sources are being depleted. This is forcing us to have to use sources that are more difficult, and thus more expensive, to reach.

76. You would look for fossils in sedimentary rocks because sediments collect and harden with the remains of animals or plants present. You would not look for fossils in igneous rocks because the intense heat that forms this type of rock would have destroyed animal or plant remains. Metamorphic rocks are not good for finding fossils because the great pressure and heat that forms this rock would have crushed and destroyed organic remains.

77. Magma, hot liquid rock deep beneath the Earth's surface, solidifies into igneous rock. This igneous rock is exposed at the surface of the Earth and is subjected to weathering and erosion. The agents of erosion break the igneous rock down into boulders which erode into smaller stones and finally into pebbles and fine sediments. The sediments become stacked layer upon layer and are compacted and cemented to form sedimentary rock.

78. A rock contains one or more minerals or mineral-like substances. Rocks are classified according to the way they form, whereas minerals are classified according to certain physical properties such as color, luster, hardness, streak, density, and crystal shape.

79. Answers may vary. Rocks are added to cement to build homes and buildings, as a base and filler for making highways, as stones for semiprecious jewelry, as decorations around flower beds of homes, and as ground cover around sidewalks.

80. Metamorphic rocks almost always form under conditions of tremendous heat and pressure—conditions not present at the surface. Metamorphism at the surface usually results from contact with lava and does not involve much change in the rock.

Contents

CHAPTER 5

Chapter Test

CHAPTER 5 ■ Weathering and Soil Formation

MULTIPLE CHOICE

Write the letter of the correct answer on the line at the left.

_____ **1.** Which of the following is an organic activity?
    a. root-pry   c. carbonation
    b. abrasion   d. exfoliation

_____ **2.** Which of the following is an example of mechanical weathering?
    a. oxidation   c. exfoliation
    b. carbonation   d. decomposition

_____ **3.** The breaking-off of sheets of rock parallel to the rock's surface is called
    a. chemical weathering.   c. exfoliation.
    b. abrasion.   d. oxidation.

_____ **4.** Material in the B horizon is
    a. topsoil.   c. partly weathered rock.
    b. unweathered parent rock.   d. subsoil.

_____ **5.** Material in the A horizon is
    a. topsoil.   c. partly weathered rock.
    b. unweathered parent rock.   d. subsoil.

_____ **6.** Weathering takes place more rapidly in areas with
    a. light rainfall and low temperatures.
    b. light rainfall and high temperatures.
    c. heavy rainfall and low temperatures.
    d. heavy rainfall and high temperatures.

_____ **7.** The most abundant minerals in soil are
    a. potassium and phosphorus.   c. granite and feldspar.
    b. nitrates.   d. clay and quartz.

_____ **8.** Weathering in which rocks are broken but *not* changed in composition is called
    a. chemical weathering.   c. carbonation.
    b. decomposition.   d. mechanical weathering.

_____ **9.** Weathering in which the mineral composition of rocks is changed is called
    a. chemical weathering.   c. exfoliation.
    b. abrasion.   d. mechanical weathering.

_____ **10.** Humus is
    a. mineral material.   c. subsoil.
    b. decaying organic material.   d. stable rock.

COMPLETION

Complete each statement on the line at the left.

_____ 1. Piles of rock fragments at the base of a mountain are called _____.

_____ 2. Weathering due to repeated freezing and melting of water is called _____.

_____ 3. A large falling movement of loose rocks and soil is called a(an) _____.

_____ 4. Soil that is moved from its place of origin is called _____.

_____ 5. _____ is the wearing away of rocks by solid particles carried by wind, water, or other forces.

TRUE OR FALSE

Determine whether each statement is true or false. If it is true, write T. If it is false, change the underlined word or words to make the statement true.

_____ _____ 1. The breaking down of rocks and other materials on the Earth's surface is called <u>weathering</u>.

_____ _____ 2. Rocks can be broken apart by changes in temperature.

_____ _____ 3. Rocks that dissolve readily in water are said to be <u>stable</u>.

_____ _____ 4. The larger the amount of exposed surface area on a rock, the <u>lower</u> is the rate of weathering.

_____ _____ 5. A cross section of soil horizons is called a <u>soil profile</u>.

USING SCIENCE SKILLS: Making Comparisons, Applying Concepts

1. Which layer is made up of subsoil? _____

2. Which layer is made up of unweathered parent rock? _____

3. Which layer is made up of topsoil? _____

4. Which layer is made up of partly weathered rock? _____

5. Which layer contains soil that has the most humus? _____

ESSAY

Write a brief paragraph discussing each of the following statements or questions.

1. Compare the textures of clay, sand, gravel, and silt. Describe which type of weathering, chemical or mechanical, can produce each of these soil particles.

_____

_____

_____

_____

_____

_____

_____

_____

_____

_____

2. Describe the role of organisms in soil formation. _____

_____

_____

_____

_____

_____

_____

_____

_____

3. Discuss three factors that determine the rate of weathering. _____

_____

_____

_____

_____

_____

_____

4. What are three ways mechanical weathering can occur? _____

_____

_____

_____

_____

_____

_____

Answer Key

MULTIPLE CHOICE

1. a **2.** c **3.** c **4.** d **5.** a **6.** d **7.** d **8.** d **9.** a **10.** b

COMPLETION

1. talus slopes **2.** frost action **3.** landslide **4.** transported soil **5.** Abrasion

TRUE OR FALSE

1. T **2.** T **3.** F, soluble **4.** F, higher **5.** T

USING SCIENCE SKILLS

1. B **2.** D **3.** A **4.** C **5.** A

ESSAY

1. Gravel particles are the largest soil particles, with a diameter between 2 and 64 mm. Gravel is broken down into sand particles, which have a diameter of less then 2 mm. Silt particles are less than 1/16 of a mm in diameter. Gravel, sand, and silt can be produced by mechanical or chemical weathering. Clay particles are smaller than silt particles and are the smallest particles in soil. They are less than 1/256 of a mm in diameter. **2.** Some organisms produce acids that cause rocks to break down chemically. Bacteria help cause decay of dead organisms. Such decaying material produces humus, which enriches soil. Burrowing organisms break apart pieces of soil and permit water to move more rapidly through the soil, which promotes weathering of underlying rock. **3.** Wetness and warmth of climate tend to speed up weathering, especially of certain types of rock. Air pollution increases the rate of weathering. The amount of time a rock is exposed at the Earth's surface affects the process. Such exposure promotes weathering. The larger the amount of exposed surface area on a rock, the faster is the weathering. Small pieces of rock or rocks with joints or cracks weather more quickly than do large uncracked rocks. **4.** Rocks can be broken apart by changes in temperature. The repeated freezing and melting of water, called frost action, is also a common cause of weathering. Root-pry can increase mechanical weathering as plant roots grow and spread out. Gravity can cause landslides in which rocks collide and break into pieces. Abrasion occurs when rocks are worn away by solid particles carried by wind, water, or other forces.

Test Bank Test

CHAPTER 5 ■ Weathering and Soil Formation

MULTIPLE CHOICE

Write the letter of the answer that best completes each statement.

_____ 1. Weathering is a process in which
    a. volcanoes extrude igneous rock.
    b. plants grow from seedlings.
    c. dew turns into frost.
    d. rock turns into sand.

_____ 2. An example of mechanical weathering is
    a. mosses dissolving away rock.
    b. acid rain eroding facial features on a marble statue.
    c. sand blown by the wind wearing away the side of a rock.
    d. rust stains turning rocks exposed to air reddish brown.

_____ 3. A concrete highway that buckles and cracks on an extremely hot day is an example of weathering caused by
    a. abrasion.   c. frost action.
    b. temperature.   d. oxidation.

_____ 4. Which of the following is not a cause of chemical weathering?
    a. oxygen   c. temperature
    b. carbonic acid   d. carbonation

_____ 5. An example of oxidation is
    a. rocks are worn away by blowing sand.
    b. carbonic acid reacts with limestone in caves.
    c. tree roots pry rocks apart.
    d. rust forms on rock that contains iron.

_____ 6. A cause of mechanical weathering is
    a. oxidation.   c. decomposition.
    b. temperature.   d. water.

_____ 7. An example of chemical weathering is
    a. a landslide.   c. frost action.
    b. sand-abraded rock.   d. iron rocks forming iron rust.

_____ 8. When frost action takes place,
    a. water turns to sleet.   c. wind wears away rock.
    b. plant roots crack rocks.   d. ice widens cracks in rocks.

_____ 9. Root pry and frost action are alike in that both
a. occur within ten days.
b. are forms of mechanical weathering.
c. are forms of carbonation.
d. occur during daylight hours only.

_____ 10. The rate of rock weathering depends on
a. the rock's color.   c. the mass of the rock.
b. minerals in the rock.   d. the volume of the rock.

_____ 11. Granite is most stable in a
a. hot, dry climate.   c. hot, wet climate.
b. cool, wet climate.   d. cool, dry climate.

_____ 12. Two rocks in the same climate weather differently when there is
a. a difference in volume.   c. no difference in temperature.
b. a difference in minerals. d. a difference in mass.

_____ 13. When carbonation occurs,
a. an acid forms.
b. wind abrades a carbon-containing rock.
c. ice splits a rock.
d. oxygen combines with a rock.

_____ 14. The first step that happens when soil begins to form is
a. thick soil develops over parent rock.
b. partially weathered rock is broken down into particles.
c. soil gets transported by the wind.
d. solid parent rock is broken into big pieces.

_____ 15. The two main ingredients in soil are
a. pieces of rock and organic material.
b. inorganic material and gravel.
c. pieces of rock and sand.
d. topsoil and gravel.

_____ 16. A sequence that correctly identifies soil particles from largest to smallest is
a. clay, gravel, silt, sand.   c. gravel, sand, silt, clay.
b. gravel, sand, clay, silt.   d. sand, gravel, clay, silt.

_____ 17. The smallest soil particle is
a. gravel.   c. sand.
b. clay.   d. silt.

_____ 18. Quartz and clay are the most abundant minerals in soil because both
a. weather very quickly.   c. are very stable.
b. contain iron.   d. minerals contain carbon.

_____ 19. Feldspars and limestone are both chemically weathered by
a. organic activity.   c. carbonic acid.
b. abrasion.   d. exfoliation.

_____ **20.** Chemical weathering can be caused by
    a. abrasion.
    b. temperature.
    c. exfoliation.
    d. water.

_____ **21.** Soil texture refers to
    a. chemical makeup.
    b. particle color.
    c. spaces between soil particles.
    d. particle size.

_____ **22.** Soil has organic material in it because
    a. the soil went through carbonation.
    b. plants and animals die and decay.
    c. it developed from frost action.
    d. iron rock weathered to rust.

_____ **23.** The type of minerals a soil has is determined by
    a. the amount of humus present.
    b. the presence of a residual soil.
    c. how quickly carbonation occurs.
    d. the rocks present.

_____ **24.** Mechanical weathering will first break rock down into
    a. silt.
    b. sand.
    c. gravel.
    d. clay.

_____ **25.** You can tell a mature soil from an immature soil because
    a. the mature soil has two horizons.
    b. immature soils have more horizons than mature soils.
    c. mature soil is more recently formed than an immature soil.
    d. mature soils have three layers.

_____ **26.** A soil horizon is different from a soil profile in that
    a. more than one soil profile makes up a horizon.
    b. soil horizons make up a soil profile.
    c. soil profiles only contain immature soils.
    d. a soil horizon contains at least three mature soils.

_____ **27.** Leaching affects soil because it
    a. makes the topsoil rich in nitrates.
    b. forces water from lower horizons to upper horizons.
    c. moves minerals from upper horizons to lower horizons.
    d. adds carbonic acid to the topsoil.

_____ **28.** In a well-formed soil profile, parent rock would be found in
    a. the second horizon.
    b. the lowest horizon.
    c. horizon C.
    d. horizon A.

_____ **29.** How would a climate with heavy rainfall and warm temperatures affect the formation of a soil?
    a. It would cause soil formation to stop
    b. It would slow down soil formation considerably
    c. It would have no effect on soil formation
    d. It would make soil weather more rapidly

_____ **30.** Which horizon consists of topsoil?
a. A horizon
b. B horizon
c. C horizon
d. D horizon

TRUE OR FALSE

Determine whether each statement is true or false.

_____ **31.** Mechanical weathering changes the chemical makeup of rocks.

_____ **32.** Acid rain is rainfall that has a concentration of sulfuric acid present.

_____ **33.** The weathering process is slowed by air pollution.

_____ **34.** Soil is formed when rocks are continually broken down by weathering.

_____ **35.** The most abundant minerals in soil are clay and granite.

_____ **36.** Loose topsoil can be washed away by heavy rainfall.

_____ **37.** A large movement of loose rocks and soil is called exfoliation.

_____ **38.** Desert regions have little weathering due to abrasion.

_____ **39.** Air and water fill the spaces between soil particles.

_____ **40.** Most chemical weathering is caused by water.

COMPLETION

Fill in the word or number that best completes each statement.

_____ **41.** The process called _____ involves the breaking down of rocks and other material present on the surface of the Earth.

_____ **42.** Decaying plant material forms _____ as it breaks down into basic substances.

_____ **43.** Sand blown by the wind against rocks causes _____, which results in the rocks being worn away in time.

_____ **44.** As mountains change with time, _____ sometimes occur as gravity pulls massive amounts of loosened rock fragments and soil down the mountainside.

_____ **45.** The weathering of rocks by the freezing and thawing of water between cracks is called _____.

_____ **46.** A classic example of weathering is the changing of iron to _____ when iron is left outdoors for a long period of time.

_____ **47.** As weathering progresses, _____ slopes, containing generous amounts of soil and rock fragments, develop at the base of mountains and hills.

_____ **48.** When a rock first breaks, its edges are _____, but weathering makes them become _____.

_____

_____ **49.** Rocks that continually break down into smaller and smaller pieces finally form _____, which provides a foundation for plants to grow.

_____ **50.** The process known as _____ causes material in rocks to be broken down into other substances.

_____ **51.** Carbon dioxide has the ability to dissolve in rainwater to form _____ acid, which can speed up chemical weathering.

_____ **52.** The type of _____ determines the kind of minerals you will have in the soil of an area.

_____ **53.** When soils develop, separate, observable _____, or layers, form from the rock that weathers in the region.

_____ **54.** A soil's _____ is determined by the size of the individual particles that make up the soil.

_____ **55.** Mature soils differ from immature soils in that they have _____ distinct layers present.

_____ **56.** Rocks that dissolve easily in water are said to be _____.

_____ **57.** When minerals in soil are washed by water from one horizon to another, the process is called _____.

_____ **58.** _____ is the process in which oxygen chemically combines with another substance.

_____ **59.** The layer of rock found beneath soil is called _____.

_____ **60.** A cross section of several horizons is called a _____.

USING SCIENCE SKILLS

Use the skills you have developed in the chapter to answer each question.

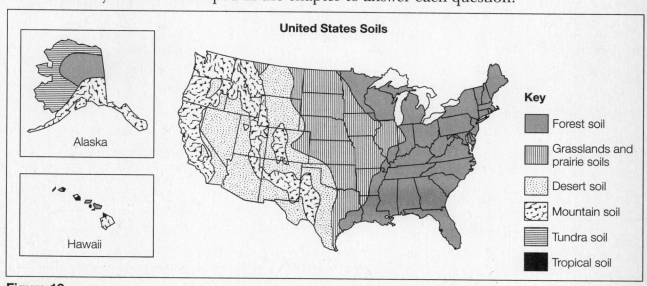

Figure 13

61. What does the key in Figure 13 show?

62. What does the map in Figure 13 show that the key does not show?

63. Using Figure 13, where are mountain soils found in the Untied States?

64. Using Figure 13, compare the soils in the eastern and central United States.

65. According to Figure 13, which of the six soils are common to all areas of our nation, including Alaska and Hawaii?

66. According to Figure 13, which soil in the United States covers the smallest area?

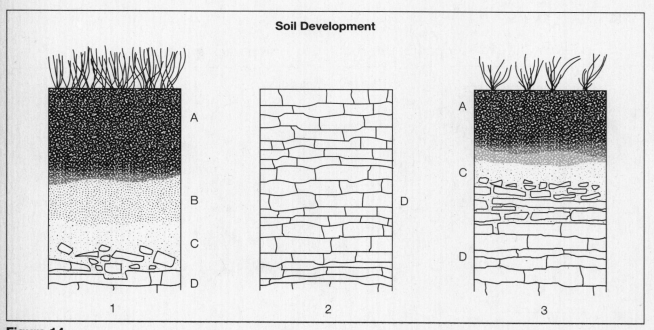

Figure 14

67. Which of the three diagrams in Figure 14 shows a mature soil?

68. Which diagrams in Figure 14 show topsoil?

69. In Figure 14, how many soil horizons are shown in diagram 1? In diagram 2? In diagram 3?

70. Name all the soil horizons shown in diagram 1 of Figure 14.

71. Which diagram in Figure 14 illustrates an immature soil? A mature soil?

72. Arrange the three diagrams in Figure 14 to illustrate the sequence in which a mature soil is formed from rock.

CRITICAL THINKING AND APPLICATION

Discuss each of the following in a brief paragraph.

73. Compare a mature soil to an immature soil.

74. How are topsoil and subsoil different from each other?

75. Prepare a written description of chemical weathering. In your description, use these words: soluble, carbon dioxide, oxidation, dissolve, lichens, and acid.

76. A cultural exchange group in New York City received a gift of an 8-m tall, 2000-year-old statue from a cultural society in Egypt. The statue, which has always been on display in the hot, dry Egyptian desert, has been permanently placed in the open air of Central Park in New York for all to see and touch. Predict what may happen to the statue.

77. Study the two diagrams shown in Figure 15. Explain how weathering is at work and what process is underway.

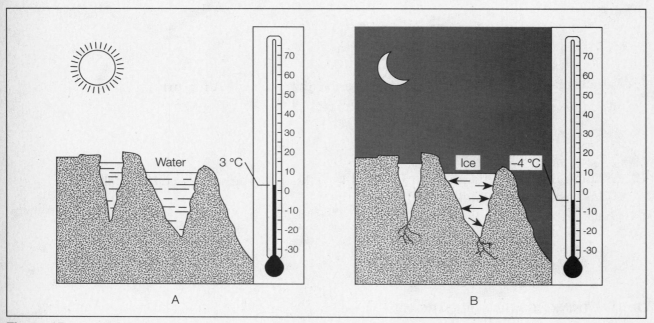

Figure 15

78. Explain two ways that temperature can weather a rock.

79. Design an experiment to find an answer to the question, "Which soil, a gravel or sand, is best at holding moisture?"

80. Match the correct effect to each of the following causes.

CAUSE	EFFECT
A._____ Leaching removes minerals.	a. These rocks are smooth and polished.
B._____ Frost action involves repeated freezing and thawing.	b. Soil in this valley does not grow corn.
C._____ Wind blows sand.	c. Cracks in rock increase with time.

81. Why are granite and marble used for tombstones? Why isn't sandstone or shale used?

82. Why does chemical weathering take place more rapidly in warm, wet weather than in cold weather?

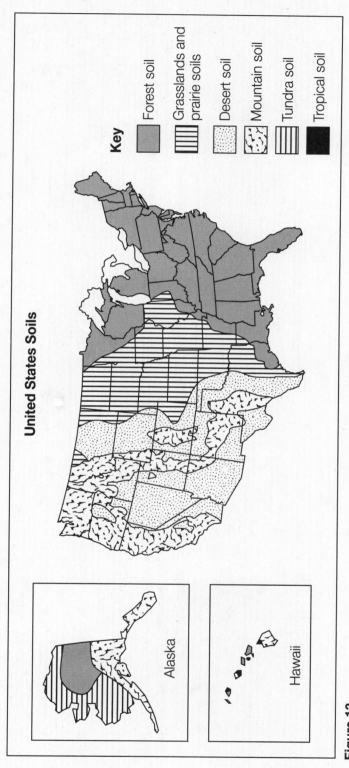

United States Soils

Key

- Forest soil
- Grasslands and prairie soils
- Desert soil
- Mountain soil
- Tundra soil
- Tropical soil

Alaska

Hawaii

Figure 13

Soil Development

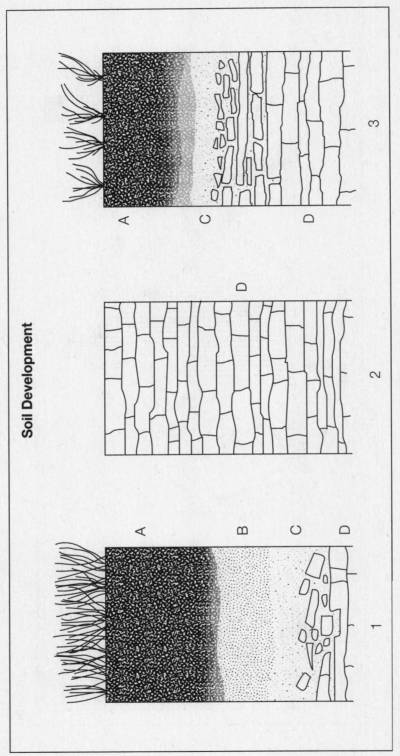

Figure 14

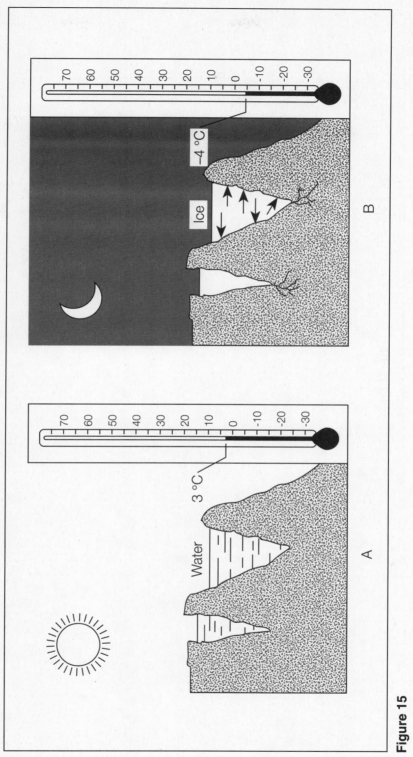

Figure 15

Test Bank Answer Key

1. d	15. a	29. d
2. c	16. c	30. a
3. b	17. b	31. F
4. c	18. c	32. T
5. d	19. c	33. F
6. b	20. d	34. T
7. d	21. d	35. F
8. d	22. b	36. T
9. b	23. d	37. F
10. b	24. c	38. F
11. d	25. d	39. T
12. b	26. b	40. T
13. a	27. c	
14. d	28. b	

41. weathering
42. humus
43. abrasion
44. landslides
45. frost action
46. rust
47. talus
48. sharp or angular; rounded or smooth
49. soil
50. decomposition
51. carbonic
52. rock
53. horizons
54. texture
55. 3
56. soluble
57. leaching
58. Oxidation
59. bedrock
60. soil profile
61. six different soil types
62. the location of the different soil types in the U.S.
63. western states, Alaska, Hawaii
64. Eastern states have forest soils while central states have grasslands and prairie soils.
65. mountain soil, forest soil
66. tropical soil
67. diagram 1
68. diagrams 1 and 3
69. diagram 1:3; diagram 2:0; diagram 3:2 (**Note:** *Parent rock is not a soil horizon.*)
70. A: topsoil; b: subsoil; c: weathered parent rock
71. diagram 3; diagram 1
72. 2, 3, 1
73. A mature soil has three layers including topsoil, subsoil, and weathered rock, whereas immature soil has only two layers.

74. Topsoil makes up the uppermost layer of soil, or A horizon. Topsoil consists mostly of humus and other organic materials and thus has many pore spaces and is dark in color. Topsoil is the most fertile part of the soil and is the site of much activity by living things. Subsoil makes up the second layer of mature soil, or B horizon. Subsoil is made up of clay and some humus, and is lighter in color than topsoil.

75. Answers may vary. One example might be: Carbon dioxide, which is soluble in water, forms a weak acid that causes limestone deposits to dissolve. Some rocks combine with oxygen. The oxidation that occurs produces oxides that wash away easily. Some rocks may have lichens attached to them. Lichens produce an acid that dissolves rock slowly.

76. Answers may vary. Since the composition of the statue is not known, one cannot be sure what the effects of the change in location will be. However, it is likely that the damp, humid New York air will have an adverse effect, as will snow and rain. Also, the statue may be damaged in time from the many hands that touch it.

77. Diagrams A and B show the mechanical weathering process of frost action. Diagram A shows water filling cracks in rock during the day. Diagram B shows the water freezing into ice at night and expanding, putting pressure on the rock, and causing it to spread apart and crack.

78. Temperature can weather a rock by repeated heating and cooling, which cracks the rock. Another way temperature weathers rock is by water freezing and thawing in the rock's cracks. As the water freezes, it expands, causing the rock to crack. Eventually the rock flakes apart.

79. Answers may vary. One experiment might be to set up two small funnels, one that contains sand, one that contains gravel. Use equal amounts of sand and gravel. Pour 100 mL of water through each funnel. Collect and measure the water that falls through each soil sample. Compare the samples and determine which soil held the most water.

80. A=b; B=c; C=a

81. Granite and marble are two types of rock that are hard and weather slowly. They are attractive and will last for long periods of time. Sandstone and shale are soft rocks that will weather away in a short period of time. They are also not as attractive as marble or granite.

82. Warm, wet climates speed up the breakdown of rock by dissolving certain minerals into soft clays. The feldspars in granite crumble into clay in warm, wet climates.

Contents

CHAPTER 6 ■ Erosion and Deposition

Chapter Test

CHAPTER 6 ■ Erosion and Deposition

MULTIPLE CHOICE

Write the letter of the correct answer on the line at the left.

_____ 1. Any material or force that moves sediments from place to place is called a(an)
   a. agent of erosion.
   b. depositional force.
   c. alluvial agent.
   d. drainage system.

_____ 2. Any process in which sediment is laid down in a new location is called
   a. weathering.
   b. deposition.
   c. erosion.
   d. mass wasting.

_____ 3. The network of runoff channels that forms a river is called a(an)
   a. tributary.
   b. drainage system.
   c. drainage basin.
   d. outwash plain.

_____ 4. A large stream that flows into a main river is called a(an)
   a. gully.
   b. rill.
   c. immature river.
   d. tributary.

_____ 5. Bends of a river that have become cut off from the river are called
   a. meanders.
   b. deltas.
   c. oxbow lakes.
   d. kettle lakes.

_____ 6. Flat areas that form on the sides of a mature river and that are sometimes covered by river water are called
   a. deltas.
   b. flood plains.
   c. alluvial fans.
   d. levees.

_____ 7. A ridge deposited along the side of a glacier is called a
   a. drumlin.
   b. terminal moraine.
   c. lateral moraine.
   d. terrace.

_____ 8. A flat platform that is formed at the base of a sea cliff is called a
   a. drumlin.
   b. terminal moraine.
   c. lateral moraine.
   d. terrace.

_____ 9. Mass wasting is caused by
   a. gravity.
   b. running water.
   c. waves.
   d. glaciers.

_____ 10. The steep side of a sand dune is called the
   a. windward side.
   b. terrace.
   c. slip face.
   d. spit.

COMPLETION

Complete each statement on the line at the left.

_____ **1.** A rapid tumbling of soil, rocks, and boulders down a slope is called a(an) _____.

_____ **2.** A river that has been developing for many thousands of years is called a(an) _____.

_____ **3.** A large mass of moving ice and snow is called a(an) _____.

_____ **4.** A hollowed-out portion of a sea cliff is called a(an) _____.

_____ **5.** The movement of water parallel to a shoreline is called a(an) _____.

TRUE OR FALSE

Determine whether each statement is true or false. If it is true, write T. If it is false, change the underlined word or words to make the statement true.

_____ _____ **1.** As a result of erosion, rills develop into <u>gulleys</u>.

_____ _____ **2.** A ridgelike deposit formed along the side of a river is called a <u>delta</u>.

_____ _____ **3.** Sediments deposited by rivers of glacial meltwater form fan-shaped areas called <u>outwash plains</u>.

_____ _____ **4.** Black sand generally comes from fragments of <u>volcanic rocks</u>.

_____ _____ **5.** Frozen pieces of glacier that have broken off and drifted into the sea are called <u>sea stacks</u>.

USING SCIENCE SKILLS: Applying Definitions

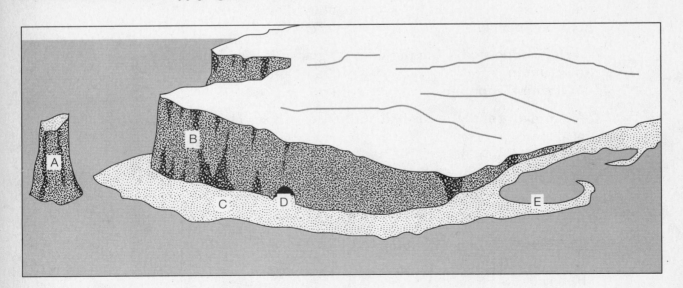

1. What is structure A called? _____

   How was it formed? _____

   _____

2. What is structure B called? _____

   How was it formed? _____

   _____

3. What is structure C called? _____

   How was it formed? _____

   _____

4. What is structure D called? _____

   How was it formed? _____

   _____

5. What is structure E called? _____

   How was it formed? _____

   _____

   What would it be called if it were entirely underwater? _____

   _____

ESSAY

Write a brief paragraph discussing each of the following statements or questions.

1. Contrast weathering, erosion, and deposition. _____

   _____

   _____

   _____

   _____

   _____

   _____

   _____

2. Explain the formation and movement of sand dunes. _____

_____

_____

_____

_____

_____

3. What are three factors that affect the amount of runoff in an area?

_____

_____

_____

_____

_____

4. Contrast an immature and a mature river. _____

_____

_____

_____

_____

_____

Answer Key

MULTIPLE CHOICE

1. a 2. b 3. b 4. d 5. c 6. b 7. c 8. d 9. a 10. c

COMPLETION

1. landslide 2. mature river 3. glacier 4. sea cave 5. longshore current

TRUE OR FALSE

1. T 2. F, levee 3. T 4. T 5. F, icebergs

USING SCIENCE SKILLS

1. sea stack; by wave erosion of a sea cliff that left a column of resistant rock 2. sea cliff; by wave erosion of a shoreline 3. terrace; by deposition of eroded material at the base of a sea cliff 4. sea cave; by wave erosion and hollowing-out of less-resistant rock in a sea cliff 5. spit; by deposition of sand by a longshore current; sand bar

ESSAY

1. Weathering is the breaking down of materials on the Earth's surface. Erosion is the process by which weathered rock and soil particles are moved from one place to another. Deposition is the process by which sediments are laid down in new locations. 2. Windblown sand is deposited near rocks and bushes, and the wind blowing over the deposits is slowed, which causes more sand to be deposited. Sand is carried up the gently sloping windward side, where the dune is built up. The sand is dropped by the wind at the crest, and falls down the steep slip face. This erosion and buildup moves the dune forward. 3. The higher the amount of rainfall, the more runoff there is, since more water is present. The more plant growth, the less runoff there is, since plant roots hold absorbent soil in place and absorb water themselves. The steeper the slope of the land, the more runoff there is, since water flows more rapidly, is absorbed less well, and also causes soil erosion. 4. An immature river is a river in an early stage of development. It cuts a V-shaped, steep-sided valley, and covers almost the entire valley floor. Its water flows rapidly sometimes in waterfalls, erodes the surroundings, and carries large particles. A mature river has developed for a long time. It flows through a broad, flat valley that is has eroded and whose walls are far from the river. It has formed meanders, has slowed down, contains few or no rapids or waterfalls, and carries small particles.

Test Bank Test

CHAPTER 6 ■ Erostion and Deposition

MULTIPLE CHOICE

Write the letter of the answer that best completes each statement.

_____ 1. When erosion occurs,
   a. lava is deposited from a volcanic vent.
   b. carbon dioxide is converted into food.
   c. vapors change into liquids.
   d. weathered rock is moved to another site.

_____ 2. Landforms are built up by
   a. leaching.   c. abrasion.
   b. deposition.   d. erosion.

_____ 3. When compared to deposition, erosion is
   a. the same process.   c. the opposite of deposition.
   b. much like deposition.   d. a support process for deposition.

_____ 4. Sediments and rocks move downhill because of
   a. heating.   c. conduction.
   b. cooling.   d. gravity.

_____ 5. An agent of erosion is a
   a. force that relocates sediments.
   b. fog that forms on the ground.
   c. material that binds sediments together.
   d. density change in a sediment that causes it to stabilize.

_____ 6. Erosion differs from weathering in that
   a. weathering carries away soil and rock.
   b. erosion splits rock and causes it to break up.
   c. erosion adds carbonic acid to soils.
   d. erosion moves materials from place to place.

_____ 7. When erosion by water occurs, the first thing that happens is
   a. sediments move downhill.
   b. water flows over land as runoff.
   c. gullies develop.
   d. rills form.

_____ 8. An agent of erosion that carries particles through the air is
   a. gravity.   c. a glacier.
   b. running water.   d. wind.

_____ 9. When mass wasting occurs,
   a. material is carried away by the wind.
   b. soil fills in rills.
   c. water wears away the base of waterfalls.
   d. soil is pulled slowly downhill.

_____ 10. The slowest type of mass wasting is
   a. soil creep.   c. mudflow.
   b. inflation.   d. deflation.

_____ 11. Which of the following is not an example of mass wasting?
   a. mudflow   c. slump
   b. landslide   d. deposition

_____ 12. An earthflow can be caused by
   a. abrasion by wind.   c. heavy rain.
   b. magma extruded as lava.   d. loess being moved by the wind.

_____ 13. When a river leaves the mountains and runs out onto a plain, it
   a. increases in speed and carries more sediment.
   b. decreases in speed and carries more sediment.
   c. increases in speed and carries less sediment.
   d. decreases in speed and carries less sediment.

_____ 14. Major changes in the shape of ocean shorelines result from
   a. a rise or drop in sea level.
   b. animals that inhabit the seas.
   c. cargo ships using open sea lanes.
   d. an alternating rise or drop in atmospheric humidity.

_____ 15. How does a spit differ from a sand bar?
   a. Spits are made of sand.
   b. Spits are parallel to the shoreline.
   c. Spits are connected to the shoreline.
   d. Spits are under water.

_____ 16. When waves come in at an angle to the shore, the water runs
   a. perpendicular to the shoreline.
   b. at an angle to the shoreline.
   c. opposite to the incoming waves.
   d. parallel to the shoreline.

_____ 17. Larger sand bars form along the shore during the winter because
   a. the cold temperatures cause sand to loosen and shift.
   b. winter waves are much larger and move more sand.
   c. winter winds blow huge amount of sand into sand bars.
   d. winter waves are smaller, allowing sand to collect into larger sand bars.

_____ 18. The kind of sand or rock particles found on a beach varies depending upon the
   a. destination of the particles.   c. streak of the particles.
   b. color of the particles.   d. source of the particles.

_____ **19.** Many Hawaiian beaches have black sand because
    a. the water reacts with the white sand, causing a color change.
    b. the sand comes from broken volcanic rocks.
    c. the same comes from eroding calcite on the islands.
    d. eroding corals form black sands.

_____ **20.** Sea terraces retard the erosion of sea cliffs because
    a. terraces allow the full force of the waves to strike the cliffs.
    b. sea cliffs are located nearest the waves.
    c. sea terraces are always located behind sea cliffs.
    d. terraces slow down waves.

_____ **21.** As stranded ice blocks left behind by a glacier melt, they form a
    a. spit.   c. lateral moraine.
    b. drumlin.   d. kettle lake.

_____ **22.** Drumlins form because
    a. snowfall changes the shape of a glacier.
    b. glaciers deposit and shape them.
    c. meltwater carries away sand and deposits it.
    d. abrasion removes soil, leaving a large cavity.

_____ **23.** Terminal moraines are located
    a. along the slow bank of a meander.
    b. along the margin where an iceberg meets the water.
    c. at the front end of a glacier.
    d. adjacent to the spit.

_____ **24.** Glaciers that slide downhill appear to move backward when
    a. less snow is deposited on the high end of a glacier.
    b. rock piles up in lateral moraines.
    c. the ice begins to move back uphill.
    d. glacier melting exceeds forward movement.

_____ **25.** A glacier is a
    a. chunk of ice that drifts in the ocean.
    b. ridgelike deposit left on a flood plain.
    c. large mass of moving ice and snow.
    d. flat area on both sides of a stream where the stream overflows its banks.

_____ **26.** Flood plain sediments are fine in size because
    a. rivers move fast across a flood plain.
    b. larer particles are deposited first along the river's sides.
    c. fine sediments settle out of rapidly moving river water first.
    d. slow-moving rivers carry a larger load than fast-moving rivers.

_____ 27. Which of the following will happen if you take a jar of water, place 100 g of mixed-size gravel in the water, close the jar, shake it, and allow the contents to settle?
   a. The fine gravel will settle out first
   b. The medium-sized gravel will rest on top of the fine gravel
   c. Coarse-sized gravel will rest on top of the fine gravel
   d. The fine gravel will rest on top of the medium-sized gravel that will rest on top

   of the coarse-sized gravel

_____ 28. The Great Lakes formed because of
   a. icebergs.   c. sea waves.
   b. wind erosion.   d. glaciers.

_____ 29. Oxbow lakes develop because
   a. rivers flow rapidly.
   b. meanders form U-shaped bends.
   c. the stream load is very high.
   d. the speed of a river increases, thereby forming a lake.

_____ 30. Drainage basins are separated from each other by a
   a. tributary.   c. flood plain.
   b. alluvial fan.   d. divide.

TRUE OR FALSE

Determine whether each statement is true or false.

_____ 31. When soil particles and weathered rock are removed from one place, the process is called deposition.

_____ 32. On deserts and beaches, the most active agent of erosion is the wind.

_____ 33. More particles are carried by the wind when it blows slowly than when it blows rapidly.

_____ 34. Loess is a mound of glacial till deposited by the wind.

_____ 35. Soil particles are held in place by plant roots.

_____ 36. Immature rivers are characterized by a U-shaped valley.

_____ 37. A large mass of moving ice in the ocean is an iceberg.

_____ 38. Erosion of sea stacks is slowed down by terraces.

_____ 39. Sea caves are formed when less-resistant rock in a sea cliff is eroded away by the action of waves.

_____ 40. In Hawaii, black beach sand develops from the erosion of volcanic rocks.

COMPLETION

Fill in the word or number that best completes each statement.

_____ 41. The process of _____ is responsible for forming the magnificent Grand Canyon.

_____ **43.** A _____ is a large mound of sand deposited by the wind near the shoreline.

_____ **44.** Farmers can stop wind erosion of their fields by surrounding them with bushes and _____.

_____ **45.** The _____ of a stream consists of the particles carried by water moving down the stream.

_____ **46.** At the mouth of a river, water deposits its sediments to form a _____.

_____ **47.** As meanders break off from a river, _____ lakes form as the ends of a meander seal off with sediment.

_____ **48.** The process by which sediments are laid down in new locations is called _____.

_____ **49.** A _____ is a large mass of ice or snow that moves down a mountain.

_____ **50.** As a glacier retreats, it deposits _____, which is composed of rocks and debris.

_____ **51.** Mature rivers usually form a _____, which appears as a large, curved loop in the course of the river bed.

_____ **52.** The Great Lakes in the northern United States were formed by the action of _____, which existed in the area long ago.

_____ **53.** When the leading edge of a glacier breaks off, it forms a(an) _____ that floats out to sea.

_____ **54.** At the shoreline, _____ cause erosion when they hit the shoreline and knock off rock fragments.

_____ **55.** The downhill movement of sediments caused by gravity is called _____.

_____ **56.** Ocean waves deposit sand and shell particles on shorelines to form a _____.

_____ **57.** As glacial ice melts, it leaves a depression or hole in the ground that fills with water and forms a _____ lake.

_____ **58.** Sediments from the Appalachian Mountains cause Atlantic beaches to have _____ colored sand.

_____ **59.** Running parallel to the shoreline, _____ currents deposit sand as they slow down.

_____ **60.** As wind blows and sand is moved, _____ may be used as a barrier to decrease erosion and assist in depositing sand.

Use the skills you have developed in the chapter to answer each question.

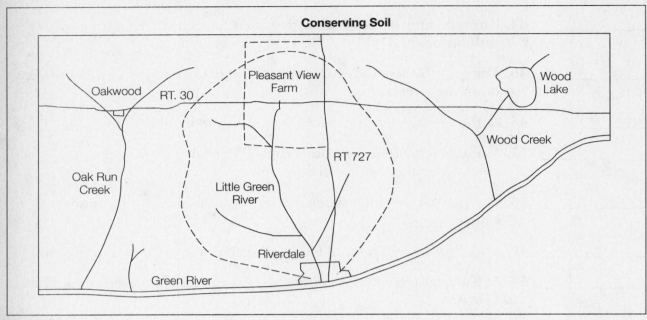

Figure 16

61. If the farmer at Pleasant View Farm in Figure 16 does not take care of his soil and erosion takes place, what effect will that have on Wood Creek?

62. As soil erosion takes place along Oak Run Creek in Figure 16, do the sediments run north and build up an alluvial fan at Oakwood? Explain.

63. How many meanders in Figure 16 are located along the Little Green River? Why?

64. Where in Figure 16 does runoff from rains on the northern part of Pleasant View Farm drain?

65. The people of Riverdale in Figure 16 are angry because the water in the river that runs through their town is loaded with brown mud and silt. As an area conservationist, where would you look for the source of Riverdale's water problem?

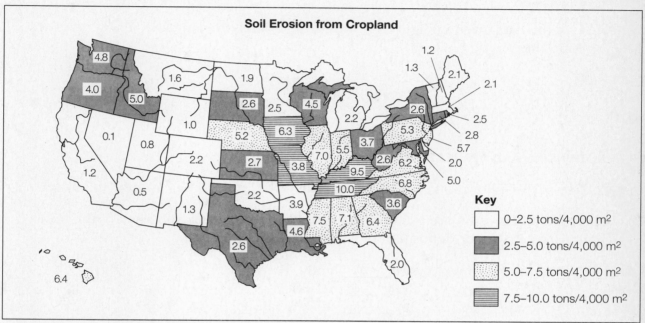

Figure 17

66. What information does the map in Figure 17 reveal about the United States?

67. Using Figure 17, how much soil on the average is lost per 4,000 square meters each year from cropland in the United States?

68. Using Figure 17, what is the lowest erosion loss incurred by a state in a year? The highest?

69. How many states in Figure 17 fall into each erosion category shown in the key?

70. How does the cropland erosion in the western United States compare to that in the eastern United States, as shown in Figure 17?

71. Based on the data given in Figure 17, what conclusions can you make about cropland erosion in the United States?

CRITICAL THINKING AND APPLICATION

Discuss each of the following in a brief paragraph, or fill in the letter of the best answer.

72. Deposition and erosion are two important Earth processes. Classify each of the following items, using "d" for deposition or "e" for erosion.

a. _____ dune

b. _____ soil creep

c. _____ slump

d. _____ loess

e. _____ gully

f. _____ mudflow

g. _____ alluvial fan

73. What is meant by stream load?

74. How does a sea cliff become a sea terrace?

75. Rivers may be either mature or immature. Each type of river has its own unique characteristics. Classify each of the following characteristics as either belonging to an immature river (i) or a mature river (m).

a. _____ carries large rocks
b. _____ lacks rapids
c. _____ river covers valley floor
d. _____ causes much surface erosion
e. _____ has meanders
f. _____ has a V-shaped valley
g. _____ carries small particles
h. _____ has an eroded valley floor
i. _____ contains waterfalls

76. Explain the difference between a lateral moraine and a terminal moraine.

77. What effect does the Continental Divide in the United States have on water runoff?

78. How are the processes of erosion and deposition different?

79. Use table salt, water, and ice cubes to design an experiment to determine if there is a difference in the exposed height of icebergs in seawater compared to fresh water. Make an outline of the steps you would use in this experiment.

80. The Mississippi River Delta is composed chiefly of mud and silt. Why are there no rocks or stones there?

81. Erosion has been wearing away the surface features of the Earth such as mountains for billions of years. If this is true, why isn't the entire surface of the Earth flat from erosion?

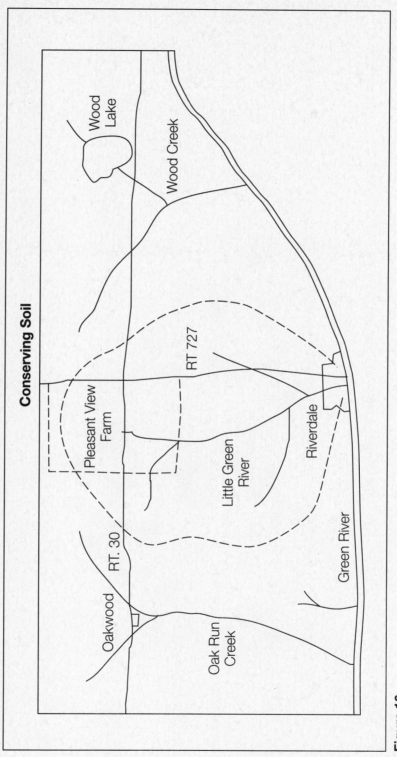

Conserving Soil

Wood Lake

Wood Creek

Pleasant View Farm

RT 727

Little Green River

Riverdale

Green River

RT. 30

Oakwood

Oak Run Creek

Figure 16

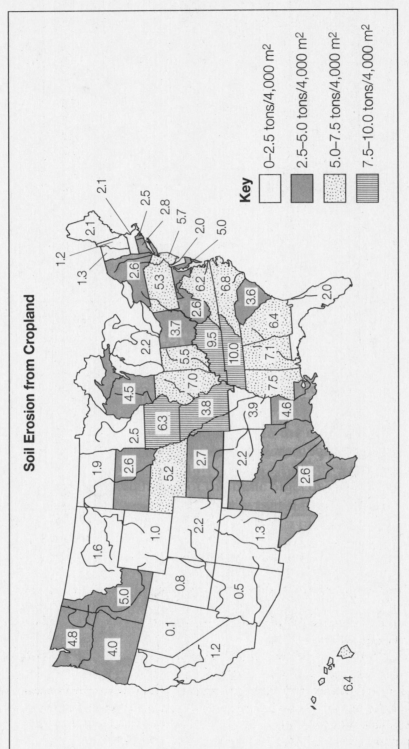

Soil Erosion from Cropland

Key

- 0–2.5 tons/4,000 m²
- 2.5–5.0 tons/4,000 m²
- 5.0–7.5 tons/4,000 m²
- 7.5–10.0 tons/4,000 m²

Figure 17

Test Bank Answer Key

1. d	15. c	29. b
2. b	16. d	30. d
3. c	17. b	31. F
4. d	18. d	32. T
5. a	19. b	33. F
6. d	20. d	34. F
7. b	21. d	35. T
8. d	22. b	36. F
9. d	23. c	37. T
10. a	24. d	38. F
11. d	25. c	39. T
12. c	26. b	40. T
13. d	27. d	
14. a	28. d	

41. erosion
42. wind
43. sand dune
44. trees
45. load
46. delta
47. oxbow
48. deposition
49. glacier
50. till
51. meander
52. glaciers
53. iceberg
54. waves
55. mass wasting
56. beach
57. kettle
58. white
59. longshore
60. windbreaks
61. Probably no effect at all because the soil would wash down into the Little Green River, not Wood Creek.
62. No. Oak Run Creek runs south and empties into the Green River; therefore sediments will empty into the Green River.
63. None because the Little Green River is an immature river that lacks meanders.
64. The runoff drains into the Little Green River.
65. You would look north of Riverdale along the Little Green River and its watershed.
66. The map reveals the amount of soil erosion that occurs per year on cropland.
67. 3.8 tons/4000 square meters
68. 0.1 ton/4000 square meters; 10.0 tons/4000 square meters
69. a. 19; b. 15; c. 11; d. 4
70. The erosion appears to be less in the west. One reason might be because there is less land planted in crops in the western states. Another reason might be because less rainfall occurs in the western United States.

71. Student answers may vary. Thirty-two states have erosion at or below the national average. Only seventeen states have erosion occurring above the national average and most of this appears to be occurring in the eastern part of the United States.
72. a. d; b. e; c. e; d. d; e. e; f. e; g. d
73. Stream load is the rock material and smaller particles carried by running water as it moves from one location to another. Large, fast-moving streams are able to carry large loads and deposit them when the stream slows down.
74. As ocean waves pound against steep shorelines, erosion cuts faces of rock called sea cliffs. As sea cliffs continue to undergo erosion by waves, the bottom of the cliff is eroded and the overhanging rocks break off, falling to the sea to form a platform around the remaining base of the cliff. This base is called a sea terrace. It will slow down erosion of other sea cliffs.
75. a. i; b. m; c. i; d. i; e. m; f. i; g. m; h. m; i. i
76. Lateral moraines are ridges of till that form along the sides of a moving glacier, while terminal moraines form as ridges of till at the leading edge of a moving glacier.
77. The Continental Divide is a ridge of high mountains running north and south across the United States. This ridge of mountains causes water runoff to move east or west of the divide. Western runoff eventually moves into the Pacific Ocean, while eastern runoff eventually moves into the Atlantic Ocean.
78. Erosion removes materials while deposition relocates materials in another location.
79. Student answers may vary. One possible experiment might be to fill two wide-mouth jars with 1 L of cold tap water. To one jar, add 30 g of table salt and stir it until it is dissolved. Add an ice cube to each jar and allow them to float in the liquid. Use ice cubes that appear to be the same size. Carefully observe how much of the ice cube floats above water level in the fresh water and in the salt water. Record your findings and remove the ice cubes. Repeat the test to accumulate more data. Compare the results you obtained and then formulate a conclusion.
80. The Mississippi River's delta lies at the mouth where the river empties into the Gulf of Mexico. The waters of the Mississippi at this point run very slowly. Slow waters are not able to carry a load of rocks and stones.
81. The Earth will never be flat due to erosion because the surface of the Earth is continually changing and being uplifted, causing new features to appear above sea level.

Contents

Performance-Based Assessment Rubrics

The Performance-Based Tests that follow provide you with an opportunity to evaluate both process skills and student understanding. Unlike methods of assessment that test factual recall, Performance-Based Tests demonstrate students' ability to *think logically*, utilize their *knowledge base*, *organize* their thoughts, and *perform basic skills* inherent to science and everyday life. Because students are not being tested on factual recall, it is important to keep in mind when scoring Performance-Based Tests that a logical and well-thought out answer can be scored just as high as the scientifically "correct" answer. Additional information on the theory behind performance-based assessment, as well as other forms of assessment such as portfolio assessment and oral reports, can be found on pages 76-77 in your Teacher's Desk Reference.

All of the Performance-Based Tests in the Prentice-Hall Science Learning System include one or more assessment objectives among the Teacher's Notes for each test. Using these objectives as the basis for evaluating skill development, the following assessment rubrics have been developed to assist you in your scoring. The rubrics allow for a range of student responses.

■ OUTSTANDING: RATING = 5

Student gives complete responses to all questions; provides a logical explanation for each response; completes all diagrams or data tables; uses descriptive terms accurately; completes the task; and demonstrates an understanding of the basic objectives.

■ COMPETENT: RATING = 4

Student gives complete responses to most questions, but is unable to provide a logical rationale for some answers; completes most diagrams or data tables; uses descriptive terms accurately; and demonstrates an understanding of the basic objectives.

■ SATISFACTORY: RATING = 3

Student gives incomplete answers to some questions and has a vague or limited rationale for answers; does not complete all diagrams or data tables; uses descriptive terms, but not always clearly or accurately; and demonstrates only a general understanding of the basic objectives.

■ UNSATISFACTORY: RATING = 2

Student provides very little response to most questions without any logical rationale for answers; does not complete most diagrams or data tables; does not use descriptive language; and does not exhibit an understanding of the basic objectives.

■ NO ATTEMPT: RATING = 1

Performance-Based Test

Test 1 The Violent Volcano

It has been a slow day. Your paper goes to press in only 5 hours and not a whiff of a story has come your way. You always thought that journalism would be exciting. People would bring bits of stories that would set you off on a search that ended on the front page. To make matters worse, the sky outside has become very black, almost as dark as night. That's all you need, a wet and miserable day. Turning on the radio to get a weather update, you tune into the middle of a serious news report and you're pretty sure that you heard the word "eruption" mentioned. Running to the window, you see that your car is covered with volcanic ash. You turn on the television to get an idea of the extent of the eruption while, at the same time, you gather your rock collection to search for volcanic samples.

Check the things in front of you to make sure you have

a piece of pumice stone and a
    selection of other volcanic rocks

Now you are ready to start.

Although you would not wish a volcano eruption to occur just for the sake of a good story, it is well timed. Before becoming a journalist, you minored in geology. This is going to be one of the best stories you have ever written.

Use your volcanic rock samples to illustrate the story (the art department will tidy up your drawings if the drawings don't turn out well). Your story should explain what volcanoes are and how they play a part in reshaping the Earth. You could explain rock formations and even bring the history of some famous volcanic eruptions into your story.

_____

_____

_____

_____

_____

_____

_____

_____

_____

DID YOU KNOW?

Approximately 7000 years ago, Mazama, a 3000-meter high volcano, located in what is now southern Oregon, erupted violently. The volcanic ash and lava flow covered the whole of the northwestern United States and part of Canada. The top of the mountain was blown away, leaving a caldera 9.8 kilometers across and about 0.8 kilometers deep. The hole gradually filled with water and is now called Crater Lake.

Performance-Based Test 1: The Violent Volcano
Teacher Notes

MATERIALS

Pumice stone and as many other samples of volcanic rock as are available.

PREPARATION

None

OBJECTIVE

Assessment of understanding of the structure of volcanoes, and the part they play in reshaping Earth's crust.

REFERENCE

Chapter 2, Earthquakes and Volcanoes

Performance-Based Test

Test 2 A Rocky Beginning

There are so many different types of rocks! You had no idea how much they differed until you started looking into their usefulness as future building materials. Architecture certainly opened your eyes to the natural world around you. You need to find out as much as possible about your rock samples and you have to develop a method to classify them.

Check in front of you to make sure you have

1. rock samples
2. balance
3. metal scraper
4. pH paper
5. graduated cylinder
6. strong magnifying glass or hand lens

Now you are ready to start.

The only way to classify rocks is to examine their characteristics and properties. Gather as much data as you can about each sample. Organize the data in a logical fashion. Gradually develop a classification system for your rock samples. Describe the tests you do as you go along. Include diagrams or drawings if they help.

_____

_____

_____

_____

DID YOU KNOW?

The greatest reported age for any scientifically dated rock is 4300 million years. These rocks were zircon crystals found 1496 kilometers northeast of Perth, West Australia. The find was reported in July 1986 by Bob Pidgeon and Simon Wilde.

Performance-Based Test 2: A Rocky Beginning
Teacher Notes

MATERIALS

three different samples of sedimentary rocks,
    igneous rocks, metamorphic rocks
balance
metal scraper
pH paper
graduated cylinder for volume measurements
strong magnifying glass (hand lens)
name cards for each rock sample

PREPARATION

Make sure that the rocks are small enough to fit into the graduated cylinder so
that the student can calculate the rock's volume and thus its density. The rocks
should be placed on top of their name cards.

OBJECTIVE

The students are to classify the rock samples using data from as many different
tests as they can develop. The students should also identify the types of rocks
and suggest uses for some of them.

REFERENCE

Chapter 4, Rocks and Minerals

Performance-Based Test

Test 3 Erosion's Effects

Nature seems determined to wash away the gentle hills in your area. In the last storm, large expanses of rocks were exposed where the soil was washed away. In other areas, last winter seems to have speeded up the breakdown of the rocks themselves. You would like to understand some of these processes and have therefore set up two experiments that will help you do so. You may also find out how sedimentary rock forms as you go along.

Check in front of you to make sure you have

1. piece of plastic gutter 2 meters long
2. small aquarium
3. supports for the gutters and aquarium
4. small pail of sandy water
5. small pail of a soil and water mixture
6. sedimentary rock sample

7. 2 large test tubes and holders
8. Bunsen burner
9. beaker with ice
10. safety glasses
11. paper towels

Now you are ready to start.

It would be too difficult to erode a hillside in the laboratory, so you have decided that the next best thing is to examine water after it has flowed over the land. Make sure that the pails are well stirred before you pour the liquids. Try pouring soil-rich water and sandy water alternately. Be careful while pouring. When you have emptied both pails, leave the tank to settle and perform the rest of your investigation. Predict what you will observe when you come back to the tank.

Use the rest of the materials available to examine the effects of changing temperatures on a piece of sedimentary rock. Give an account of what you do, including diagrams. Later, you can see if what you have done helps you understand the erosion of the hillsides that is taking place near you.

_____

_____

_____

_____

_____

_____

_____

Using evidence from your experiment, can you explain weathering and erosion?

_____

_____

_____

_____

_____

DID YOU KNOW?

In 1985, a mud slide in the town of Armero—a town of 25,000 inhabitants near the volcano Nevado Del Ruiz, Colombia—killed about 23,000 people. The mud, traveling at 100 kilometers per hour, flowed into the town covering the houses so that only their roofs could be seen. The disaster followed a series of minor earthquakes and eruptions of the volcano, but in spite of all the warning signs, and the fact that mud slides were fairly common in the area, nobody had ordered the evacuation of the town.

Performance-Based Test 3: Erosion's Effects
Teacher Notes

MATERIALS

piece of plastic gutter 2 meters long
small aquarium
supports for the gutter and aquarium
small pail of sandy water
small pail of soil and water
sedimentary rock sample that will fit into the test tube
2 large test tubes and holders
Bunsen burner
beaker with ice
safety glasses
paper towels

PREPARATION

Mix the materials in the two pails so that the water and sediments will flow easily. Set up the gutter so that water flows down it into the aquarium. Make sure it is possible to surround the large test tubes completely with ice when they are placed in the beaker.

OBJECTIVE

The students' ability to deduce facts from a laboratory experiment and apply them to natural processes is being assessed. They will also have to organize the work to enable them to complete the tasks.

REFERENCES

Chapter 5, Weathering and Soil Formation
Chapter 6, Erosion and Deposition